Ghosts of the Gate City
Hauntings in Denison, Texas

Brian C. Hander

CONTENTS

Dedicated to all of those who shared their stories with me. Your stories made this whole project possible and for that, I am incredibly grateful.

Introduction

Denison has one of the most unique and vibrant histories of any city in Texas. Founded in 1872 by hardworking men and women, the Gate City of Texas has continued to flourish for the past 146 years. Today, our city boasts many unique buildings, both old and new, that celebrate our history and tell our stories.

The purpose of this book is two-fold in nature. My primary goal is to relate ghost stories and local legends as they have been reported and passed down through generations. Secondly, I hope to give readers a better understanding of the history of some of our haunted locales. The more understanding we have of the awe-inspiring history around us, the better we can work to preserve our sense of place and unique character that comes from the places surrounding us.

Some of these stories have been corroborated and others have simply been passed down with no true proof to back them up. I make no promises as to the validity of any of the ghost stories; I simply wrote down what I had learned through interviews and research.

One thing I would also like to make very clear is that some of these stories take place at residences and businesses, and the buildings' owners deserve respect. Please do not trespass onto any of the properties that have been named in this book; they are all private properties and deserve to remain as such.

I owe a huge debt of gratitude to the following individuals: Melanie and Matt Truxal, Cindy Truxal, Janet Fry, Elsie Russell, Kim Huff, Gary Sewell, Paul and Kim Ontiveros, John and Michelle Apodaca, and Natalie Curtis. Your stories and information gave this book so much life. You all were so wonderful to share your experiences with me.

To my wife, Erin, thank you for supporting me while I wrote this book. Only you would put up with me when I would scare myself with all of these stories. A huge thank you to my wonderful editors and proofreaders: Melanie Truxal, Ashly Schomer, and Megan Cochran. You all helped make this book a cohesive work and saved me from many frightening spelling and grammar errors.

Finally, any errors are mine and mine alone. Many hours went into this book, and I made every effort to record the facts as they were presented to me; however, being human there are bound to be errors throughout a work of this size. I hope you enjoy this book, learn some of our unique history, and get a better understanding of the spirits that linger around our beautiful city.

Brian Hander
October 2018

Chapter One

Denison's First Hauntings
Haunted from the Beginning

Denison is not an old city by Southern standards, yet its hauntings rival that of cities such as New Orleans, Savannah, and Charleston. While these cities were conceived in the 17th and 18th centuries, Denison had its beginning a little later in 1872. Our city was founded as the terminus for the ever-expanding Missouri, Kansas, and Texas Railroad.

The Denison Town Company was formed to plat out the town and sell lots to new, prospective citizens. The city quickly grew to several thousand inhabitants with all manner of business houses and elegant homes. Everything seemed poised for the city to have endless success for all, but dark forces were at play from the very beginning.

The Haunted Traveler

One early local newspaper, The Denison Daily News, reported Denison's first haunting on July 29, 1874. The paper reported that a recent resident of the city had been haunted by a ghostly spirit that followed him to "every town, hamlet, and village" in which he attempted to locate. The ghost followed him from Ohio, through Missouri, and caught back up with him again in Texas.

The more he attempted to allude the spirit, the more violent she became, finally attacking him along the highway outside of town. The man claimed he was headed to Mexico as the States had become too much of a hot spot for him. It was hoped that the ghost would follow him and leave our city, but the man was never reported of again, leaving one to wonder if the spirit still lingers.

The Hauntings of 1876

Hauntings in Denison have always been a prevalent part of society. Reports of ghosts, spirits, and haunted houses have been present since the first newspaper started publishing in the fledgling town. One instance appeared in the *Denison Daily Cresset* on May 6, 1876, just four years after the founding of Denison.

The Cresset reported that a haunted house was situated in the neighborhood of the M, K & T Railroad stockyards. The report stated that strange noises were heard throughout the home, and that the ghost of an African American woman walked the halls carrying a tallow candle in her hand. She would walk around the house and would suddenly disappear up the chimney as if nothing more than a puff of smoke.

The M,K &T Stockyards from an 1876 map of Denison. The stockyards were located south of Fores t Park along Rusk Avenue.

Faces were known to appear in the windows, even when no one was in the home. Along with all of the noise that was heard throughout the house, furniture would sometimes be thrown about the rooms. The structure was one of the oldest homes in Denison and it was supposed that a foul deed had been committed within its precincts at some time or another.

Denison Birds Eye View Map fromm 1876

Another haunted house cropped up in October of 1876. The article appeared in the *Denison Daily Cresset* on October 28, 1876 and stated the following:

A Haunted House

"We are in possession of the greatest sensation that our city has ever experienced- a haunted house. At the request of the parties living there, we refrain from giving any particulars or names at the present time. Within the last twenty-four hours a number of prominent citizens have visited the premises and were nonplussed at what they saw and heard. A little girl about eight years old became entranced

last evening, and wrote spirit messages. In her usual condition, she is unable to write at all.

Loud knocks in the building that can be heard in the neighborhood, are heard all over the house. Everything has been done to discover if there is any trickery. The front stoop was taken up last evening; pistol shots have been fired where the knocking is heard, but all remains a mystery. A Cresset reporter has been invited and will visit the premises this evening."

An article appeared the next day in the *Cresset*, and apparently, the house was so sensational and made for such great news, that the identity was revealed. The article reads:

The Haunted House

"The haunted house sensational article, which appeared in the evening paper, Saturday, awakened no little curiosity and the result was that fully a hundred persons collected around the house after dark, (Mr. Jacob McLaughlin's residence, corner of Gandy Street and Burnett Avenue) while a goodly number crowded inside. Though the dining room table was brought forth, a circle formed and Burhans, master of ceremonies, invoked the spirits repeatedly to 'please rap,' there was nary a rap, or at least none had been heard up to 10 o'clock, when the writer left."

Jacob McLuaghlin owned a saloon (the name has been lost to history) in the heart of the red-light district at the northwest corner of Skiddy Street (now Chestnut Street) and Austin Avenue. The current site is occupied by a law firm, and the original structure is no longer extant.

The map shows the intersection of Gandy St. and Burnett Ave. in 1876. The intersection is located at the center of the map, the haunted house shows a cruciform-style house at the northwest corner of the intersection.

His home was located at the northwest corner of Gandy Street and Burnett Avenue, which is now occupied by a home in the Craftsman Bungalow style. While this is a newer home, it was common to simply add on to existing structures or remodel them in period styles, so it is a possibility that part of the original haunted house still exists.... leaving room for the possibility that the home site is still haunted to this day.

A few years later, the same address would appear in the news once again. The story is as follows:

"There was excitement at reports sent out that the residence owned by the Cuff Bros., corner of Gandy Street and Burnett Avenue, was haunted. It had been proclaimed by Tom Foley, who lived there, that in the night, noise, and violent knockings on the floor, prevented

sleep; and Mrs. Foley declared that she had on several occasions seen a sad, pale-faced woman in the room, that, when approached, faded into the wall. The entire newspaper force of the city press spent one night there. They all got drunk and raised such a racket that, about midnight, they were invited to get out and go home, or the police would be called to eject them."

The current home located at the northewest corner of Gandy St. and Burnett Ave.

From the articles, we can infer that the house was haunted for a number of years, and that the hauntings occurred to several different owners. While no more has ever cropped up about hauntings at the site, it is still a possibility that whatever spirit possessed the home still lurks within its walls.

The Texas Street Ghost

The hauntings returned to Denison just after the dawn of the 20th century. On November 24, 1901, *The Sunday Gazetteer* reported the following:

"Stories of weird doings and ghostly escapades at a house on Texas Street have been circulated the past week. The stories, nearly all of which are attested to by responsible parties, are incredible, and the person who hears for the first time the wonderful activities of the invisible spirits, or whatever it is, only shakes his head in doubt.

Three weeks ago, the first weird manifestation of many was given to the lad. The boy was in the back yard shooting at birds with a rubber sling shot, when the weapon was suddenly snatched from his hand. The lad looked in vain for the person who had robbed him.

The boy's mother was working in the house the day following her son's strange experience, when she heard a noise coming from the cupboard in which she keeps her canned fruit. Throwing open the doors she saw the glass jars dancing up and down. As she looked in the jars stopped the jig.

A neighbor was invited to dinner last Sunday a week ago. As he prepared to hang his hat on a nail, he was warned that it would no be safe there. In a joking manner, he laid his hat on a chair and sat on it. When he got up from the table, his hat was missing.

The writer has been investigating ghost stories-Denison ghost stories-for the past 25 years and yet after thorough and impartial investigation we have never been able to see or hear anything mysterious. The Texas Street ghost story when sifted down will coincide with the rest of our past experiences."

Located at 700 West Texas Street. This home, built ca. 1890, was the likely haunted house discussed in the 1901 article.

Just two years after this article was published, the newspaper would again take up the topic of a haunting on Texas Street, this one at a different home. The site contained a cabin that was occupied by an African American family with the last name of Yarbrough. A man was murdered in the home, or was, at the very least, reported to have been taken to the home after he was murdered.

The cabin was described as haunted, and no one would live there. B.C. Murray, editor of the paper, reported that one of the manifestations was the pulling up and down of the well buckets; moreover, rocks were thrown against the cabin, and heart-stopping groans could be heard coming from within the walls of the structure.

A Mr. Dickinson, said to be a truthful and reliable citizen, stayed in the home one night and said that the stories were true. He did indeed witness the moving of the well bucket and the constant thumping as if rocks were thrown against the cabin. Deeming the location uninhabitable, the neighbors set the house ablaze in hopes of removing the spirit from the neighborhood.

The Woodard Street Spirit

The *Sunday Gazetteer* reported the following in an article titled, "Ghost Stories" on July 3, 1910:

"Here is a story that is true, and vouched for by person at present living here. The information is furnished by the wife of the city editor, who is calculated to tell a straight story without any flights of imagination.

The manifestations happened at the home of Mrs. Brown, who was then a teacher in the public school and resided in the 500 block Woodard Street.

A little girl, who was in the primary department of the public school and had not as yet acquired the practice of writing, was stopping with Mrs. Brown. At an early hour of the evening, a noise was heard like someone knocking for admission. The front door was opened, and no one was there. The knocks were repeated on the window and at various points on the outside of the house.

Mrs. Brown called in the neighbors, and the outside of the house was surrounded, but still the manifestations continued. The yard and premises were thoroughly searched, but no person could be discovered. Frequently violent knocking was heard on the roof.

The little child, who had been asleep in the bed, opened her eyes and then apparently relapsed into a trance, with deep breathing. She finally called for paper and pencil, and wrote in a plain hand, so that all present could read, message after message that was signed by what purported to be her mother, who had been dead for some time.

It must be recollected that the child in her normal state could not write at all. The mother did not want her little girl forgotten, as the holidays were near at hand. She (or whatever it was) laid great stress on the request that the child should receive presents. The child wrote a number of messages, her hand seeming to be under the control of some invisible spirit.

During the time the child was writing, the knockings continued all over the house. George Strobe (dead for many years) entered the house, and when told of the manifestations, said, 'Well; it must be a d---d poor spirit that can't make more noise than that.' Or words to that effect. In an instant it seemed as if large stones were being hurled on the roof, and the residence fairly vibrated.

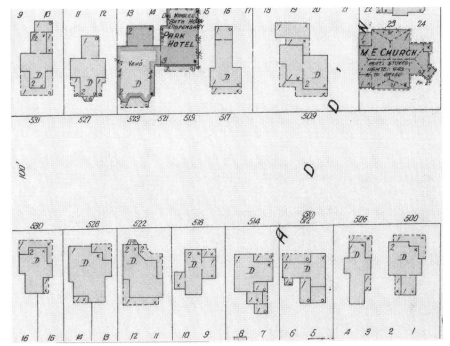

The 500 block of Woodard Street, ca 1908.

Mrs. Pollard, who resided a block distant and was a great believer in spiritualism, was sent for. When the lady appeared on the scene, the situation was explained. She declared that it was the spirit of the child's mother who was communicating.

The pencil finally dropped from the child's hand; she opened her eyes widely, and the demonstration ended. The next day she was taken to Mrs. Pollard's residence, and the "spirits" were invoked but with no manifestations whatever.

On what hypothesis the manifestations at Mrs. Brown's residence can be explained, we offer no explanation. Here was a child about four years old, that had never written a line in her life, and yet through some unknown agency she wrote rapidly and correctly, and in letters so plain that it was read without any difficulty whatsoever.

There are other stories of haunted houses, but the one that happened at the home of Mrs. Brown was literally true."

Typical homes found in the 500 block of West Woodard (dating from the early 1900's) that could have served as the site of the haunting.

Chapter Two

Denison's Bloody Fourth
A Glorious, Tragic, Gala-Day of Horror

A bright, sunny day on July 4, 1879, began as a glorious day for many, but ended in the deaths of three men and a fourth wounded so badly that he died days later from an infection. Among the victims was Denison's esteemed constable, who was shot in the line of duty.

Estimations from that day said that nearly 1,000 strangers began arriving in Denison as early as July 3 by horseback, wagons, and on foot to join in the Independence Day celebrations. The Knight of Pythias, the Denison Cornet Band, and the Gate City Guards waited at the depot to welcome those travelers arriving by train.

A.R. Collins, a local real estate agent, was grand marshal and the Goddess of Liberty was Jeanette Kirk, representing the ideal of American liberty. A grand parade took place and Georgiana, the beloved pet of the fire department, lay full length on top of the truck sponsored by the Junior Fire Company. Miss Edith Doak was adorned in red, white and blue as she sat under a canopy on the Hook and Ladder Company's display.

Others in the procession included chiefs of the Sherman, Dallas, and Denison Fire Departments, local baseball clubs, archery clubs, orator of the day, mayor and city council, an African American band, merchants and mechanics with displays on wagons, as well as citizens in carriages and visitors on horseback. The parade was so large that even the Chickasaw Nation sent a delegation to join.

The procession wound its way around Forest Park through thousands of happy spectators and elaborately decorated private residences along the parade route. American and Texas flags were flying proudly from homes and businesses alike, including the boot and shoe store of M.H. Sherbourne and the business house of Harry Tone.

While all of the excitement and parades were occurring at Forest Park, a more sinister event was taking place not far away on Main Street. The following is a reprinted article from the July 4, 1879 edition of the *Denison Daily News* detailing the events of that day. It has been written exactly as it appeared including spelling and context.

Forest Park as it appeared in Denison's early days.

"The Fourth of July will be remembered in more respects than one, three terrible murders being committed on that day in our city.

The incidents attending the death of Constable Nelms are almost too painful for recital. It is the old story, a six-shooter in the hands of a notorious desperado, infuriated by whiskey.

Charley Russell, a mulatio, well known here as a desperate character, and who should have been hung in Missouri several years ago, if all reports are true, shot and killed Constable Nelms, one of the bravest and most gallant officers in the State of Texas.

There are so many reports in circulation concerning the terrible tragedy, that it is difficult to ascertain the facts of the shooting.

Russell, who has charge of a farm belonging to Mr. Alec Reddick, northwest of the city, arrived in town on horseback on the morning of the fourth. During the day, Russel hung around the Bank Exchange, drinking quite frequently, his potations making him quarrelsome and dangerous.

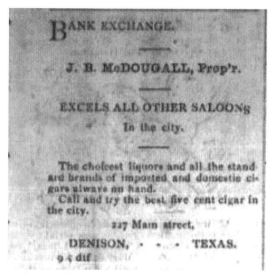

An early advertisement for the Bank Exchange Saloon at 227 West Main Street.

In the afternoon a large crowd of people were in the saloon drinking, many being drunk. A disturbance took place between a railroad man and an Indian. During the progress of the quarrel Russel interfered, crying in an excited manner, 'I am the chief. I can whip any man in the house.' The railroad man then struck Russell, who in return knocked him down.

It looked very much just then, as if the fight would become general, the crowd becoming terribly excited. During the excitement, the railroad man, unobserved, procured a mallet with which he dealt Russel a blow on the side of the head, causing the blood to run from his ear.

John McDougall, the proprietor of the saloon, and Alec Reddick, then endeavored to have Russell leave the premises, Reddick calling on Constable Nelms to arrest him. Russell by this time had been pushed by the crowd from the saloon out of the door into the back yard. Constable Nelms told Russel that he was under arrest.

Russel was grasped by the arm by McDougall, who said, "Go!" shoving him into the alley. Russel went over to Gheen's wagon yard, and procuring a revolver returned to the saloon. He commenced discharging the revolver as he entered the back leading to the saloon. On the approach of Russell the crowd in the saloon fled in dismay out the front door. It is supposed that at this time Charley Colbert was shot, he being, as he says, in the saloon half-asleep.

Constable Nelms in the meantime, supposing the Russell was endeavoring to escape when he saw him leaving the premises by the back door, rush out of the saloon to Rusk Avenue, and thence into the alley, entering the saloon at the back entrance. Russell was waving his pistol when Constable Nelms entered. Mr. Nelms said, "Charley, I want you," or words something to that effect. Leveling his pistol at Nelms, Russell answered, "I will never be arrested today; tomorrow I will surrender." Constable Nelms then fired, unfortunately missing his man.

The Negro advanced towards Constable Nelms, leveled his pistol over McDougall's shoulder, and fired, the ball taking effect in his head a little above the left eye, killing him almost instantly. Russel shouting, "I am the boss-I am the chief," retreated into the back yard to the alley to Rusk Avenue. Standing in front of Gheen's livery establishment, he flourished his revolver, defying the crowd to come and arrest him.

227 West Main (two-story building at right) ca 1895

After standing there for a moment, he walked up Rusk Avenue to Main Street, going up into the second story to the front room of the Bank Exchange.

At this moment the excitement was something terrible to behold, and will never be forgotten, at least by our reporter. The crowd was swaying to and fro, the majority with drawn revolvers, calling for vengeance on the murderer of Constable Nelms. For a moment, no one dared go up the stairway in pursuit of Russell. Ex-deputy Sheriff Massey was the first to mount the stairway, with revolver in hand, followed soon afterwards by two or three others, Marshal Sam Ball, of Sherman being one of the number.

Mrs. Nelms, the mother of the deceased, hearing of the death of her boy, left home in Crawford Street, and went into the saloon where he lay on the floor, the blood oozing from a ghastly wound in the head.

The mother took the gory head of her son into her arms, calling down the vengeance of heaven on his murderer.

About five minutes or perhaps longer, after Ex-Deputy Sheriff Massey went up the stairway, several shots were fired. In the meantime, Dick and Harry Nelms, brothers of the deceased, along with their father, all armed, appeared on the street. Dick Nelms rushed up the stairway, and in a moment or so, two other pistol shots were heard.

Marshal Sam Ball, of Sherman, then appeared at the front window stating that Russell was killed. This intelligence was received with evident satisfaction by the dense multitude who cheered lustily. The local of the news was one of the first to see Russell, as he lay on the floor, hardly distinguishable for the blood on his face. His head was riddled with bullets.

Who fired the fatal shot, killing Russell, it is not positively known. Mr. Jim Massey, is, however, supposed to be the individual who did the charitable act. As soon as the excitement subsided, Russell's body was dragged down the stairway, thrown on a cart and taken away.

Mr. Nelms' body was conveyed to the residence of his father on Crawford Street, where immense numbers of sorrowing friends viewed the remains.

"Dust to Dust"

The funeral took place from the residence of his father, J.H. Nelms, on Crawford Street, at 2 o'clock p.m. Saturday. A pathetic discourse was delivered by Rev. Mr. Parks, of the Baptist Church, in which he feelingly alluded to the high estimation in which Mr. Nelms was held as a faithful and efficient officer. At the sacrifice of his life, he endeavored to act up to his oath of office, and fell at his post, a martyr to duty. The funeral procession was one of the longest ever seen in Denison.

The scene at the tomb was affecting in the extreme. As the body was being lowered to its final resting place the heart of the aged father could no longer subdue its burden of grief, and he gave vent to his feelings in an outburst of anguish that brought tears to the eyes of all present. And the expression of grief on the part of the stricken wife, mother and sister were even more heart-rending.

Jim Nelms was recognized by all who knew him as a warm-hearted generous man, and at home, from all accounts, he was even more remarkable for his amiable qualities. We feel that we are but expressing the wishes of all the good people in the city in extending for them their sincere sympathy with the family in their great bereavement.

Murder No. 3

On the morning of the fourth, the body of an Indian named Napoleon Anderson, a son of Captain Anderson, who lives in the Chickasaw Nation, near Tishomingo, was found in the rear of Wolf's saloon with two bullet holes in his head. Parties living in the vicinity heard the shooting, and saw two mounted men ride away.

It is said by Anderson's neighbors that he was a desperate character, having killed two or three persons in the Territory. It is supposed that the murder was committed by some of the friends of Anderson's victims. The body was sent to the Territory by Gov. Burney."

The newspaper article ended at this point. The entire time these events unfolded, the festivities continued in Forest Park because the participants, thinking they were hearing fireworks, were unaware of the Main Street massacre.

Charley Colbert was taken to his home across the Red River, where his family tried to care for him. However, Charley's wound proved too damaging and became infected. Within a few days he would die, bringing the death toll to four.

227 West Main as it appeared in the 1950's. The building was demolished in the late 1950's to make way for the expansion of the Citizen's Bank.

Thus ended one of Denison's deadliest days along the booming and bustling Main Street. While there have been no direct hauntings related to this day, it is possible that the spirits of the murdered still linger along Denison's historic commercial strip. While business owners have always reported strange occurrences, they are normally attributed to the spirits of former shop owners or residents. Is it possible that some of the hauntings are the work of those killed on that fateful Independence Day?

Chapter Three

Monsters on Main
What Lies Behind the Historic Facades

Downtown Denison, the core from which all commercial and residential growth has flowed, is affectionately known as the heart of the city.

While it was the beginning for our city and many of her residents, it was also where many lived out their final days and moments…leading some to believe that these "oldest residents" still hang around throughout the shops and restaurants of the central business district.

The 100 block of West Main as it appeared in 1877.

500 West Main

One site that has remained active throughout the years is 500 West Main, the current home of Main Street Mall. The original site housed the first Hotel Denison, which will be discussed later in this book. While the current structure was built from the 1930's to 40's, the site has a long history that extends nearly as far back as the founding of Denison.

The main ghost currently residing at the site is known affectionately as "Miss Shirley," so named for Neil and Mary Shirley who were prominent citizens in the community and operated a furniture store, known as Jennings Furniture, at the site for a number of years.

While the building eventually changed ownership, many believe that Mary never left. Employees have felt a rush of cold air in different parts of the building followed by the image of Miss Shirley appearing. She is known to appear, float across the room, and disappear into the wall as if she was never even there.

View of the 500 block of West Main Street in the 1940's-1950's. The site of Main Street Mall is at front right.

One instance that took place involved a customer turning to ask a question to what she thought was an employee of the store. Instead, she turned face to face with what she described as a woman who simply vanished into thin air when she made eye contact.

While some strange events have happened on the bottom floor, most of the activity seems to be limited to the third floor, which is mainly used for storage and is not currently open to the public. Of note, many of the items stored in the third floor belonged to the Shirley's, including personal items such as photos and letters.

Miss Shirley has always been described as a friendly presence rather than the more sinister ones that appear in most Hollywood films. Local business owners are still holding out hope that Miss Shirley will help them move heavy furniture to the second-floor showroom.

Main Street Mall as it appears today at 500 West Main Street.

There are some that believe that spirits remain from the days when the building housed a funeral home and mortuary. One employee described felling an energy in the first floor while he was there.

Suddenly a figure floated through, described as a young, petite, woman in gray and white with a small Victorian coat on. He did not get a good look at her face, but said she floated across the room and disappeared into a nearby

311 West Main

The building at 311 W. Main Street has a long and varied history in Denison. At the time the address was first mentioned in 18 75, a doctor who specialized in surgeries on women and children utilized the building for his practice.

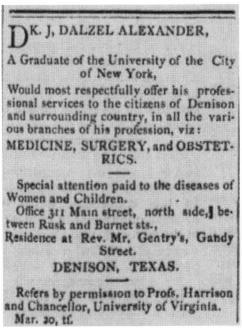

An early advertisement for Dr. Alexander, a local physicain and surgeon.

The building later housed a succession of dentists and surgeons before opening as a tailor shop, owned by the "fashionable cutter" J.M. Hill. Mr. Hill remained in operation for a number of years before closing his shop and moving from the city.

In 1883, an enterprising woman by the name of Mrs. S.D. Parkinson began operation of a millinery at the site, where she made some of the most beautiful hats that had ever been seen in the city. Her much sought after apperal was often featured in the local newspaper.

Mrs. S. D. Parkinson has opened up a nice line of millinery at 311 Main street, where she would be pleased to see the ladies of Denison who are wanting anything in the hat and bonnet line. She makes frames to order, and guarrantees perfect satisfaction.

Mention of Mrs. Parkinson's millinery shortly after its opening in 1883.

Other various businesses housed within the building included a butcher, barbershop, meat market, noted local architect Pierre Lelardoux, Dollarhide and Harris general store, the Eagle Drug Store, and Peterson's Hardware. Most recently, the building has been refurbished to house the popular 2 Chicks Home and Market.

The owners and vendors at the store have witnessed strange phenomenons, most usually that items in the store seem to move each night. Signs would also be turned over, and it was not uncommon for doors to open and close on their own.

One day, a porcelain hand figurine was found broken on the floor. Suspecting foul play, camera footage was reviewed to hopefully catch whoever had been disturbing the items. In the footage, a kind of fog, described sometimes as a mist, creeps into the store from the back rooms and as the fog approaches an item on the shelf, the item is thrown to the floor. The fog-like energy remained in the store for about 45 minutes before dissipating.

Upon inspection, there was no gas leak nor was there any other explainable reason for why the fog would appear in the video. No fans were left on and the item was placed firmly on the shelf. Business owner, Elsie Russell, has named the spirit Jack after one of the building's former owners.

Reports have also been made of Jack touching one of the booth owners. She was at the store by herself and could feel a presence, but thought nothing of that as Jack is normally always present. However, she was soon shocked when a hand went along her back, although no one else was in the store! She quickly left and tries to avoid being left alone at the store from now on.

There never seems to be a dull moment anymore at the store, as the hauntings have become more frequent, although Elsie seems to have scared the spirit somewhat as no more items have been broken. The footage of the mist is available on social media, so be sure to check it out, and then see if you can spot Jack around the store when you shop.

321 West Main

The *Sunday Gazetteer* reported that there used to be a house on Main Street, where the present building at 321 West Main sits, that was haunted. The house was located in the rear of Mr.

Pollard's tin shop and all sorts of strange occurrences happened.

Every evening around dusk, footsteps could be heard ascending the stairway on the east side of the building and connecting with the second story. Several residents who lived in the building moved away, claiming they could hear the invisible steps going up the stairway.

A man by the name of Mr. Charles Fillmore, a cashier for the Katy Railroad, was a tenant of the second floor of the building. Fillmore made a public statement that, about midnight one night, something entered his through his securely fastened door, and that he could hear chairs moving and footsteps in the room.

The following morning he discovered that the chairs had indeed been moved and that his washbowl and pitcher had been placed on the floor. Normally open to spiritualism, Fillmore was so upset that he ultimately ended up vacating the space.

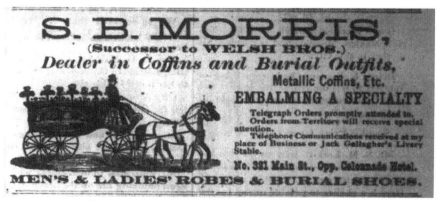

An early advertisement for an embalming specialist at 321 W. Main.

At one time, the site was host to the S.B. Morris Company, boasting specialties in embalming. It was thought that one of the poor souls who traveled through that doorway never left. Local lore also states that an old, eccentric man had died in the second floor of the building. He had come to Denison a stranger and would never give any information into who he was or where he came from, though he did leave some money upon his death.

A view of 321 West Main from te late 1800's. The building is located at left center with the three centered windows in the façade.

The building would pass through a succession of owners housing everything from a general store to antique shops. It is said that one of the neighboring store owners in more recent times took up dark magic and opened what neighboring businesses claim to be a "doorway" into the underworld.

321 West Main Street as it appeared in 2013.

While nothing recent has been reported by the owners of the current store, A Timeless Journey Vintage Boutique, the possbility always lingers that the site is still active.

Is it possible that this "doorway" awakened the entity responsible for the haunting that took place over a century ago?

118 West Main

Located at 118 West Main, the building occupied by Vitina's Deli sits on one of the oldest commercial sites in Denison's history. With the depot only a block away, businesses chose this block as prime real estate due to the ease of access travelers could utilize when riding the numerous trains through town.

The building served primarily as an early day real estate office and auction house and was originally a one-story stone building with a basement. Early day buildings in Denison were commonly built of wood and not meant to last, so the fact that this one was stone was significant as it was truly built to stand against the tests of time.

In the 1880's the building was purchased by merchant tailors, Werneburg and Son, a popular enterprise from Galveston. A massive remodeling effort took place in order to add flair to the building that the owners were so fond of seeing amongst Galveston's Victorian commercial blocks.

The iron columns that were added as part of the remodel are still on the building today and were the first ever cast in this city. They were made by J.B. Roger's foundry with designs from Joseph Schott, a prolific Denison architect. During the remodeling, a new facade was attached to the building and a second floor was constructed on top of the original structure.

118 West Main Street as it appeared in 1984. Building is at center with four windows on second floor.

When completed, the structure was one of the most opulent buildings in the city and an incredible addition to the 100 block of Main Street. High profile men such as J.J. Fairbanks made their offices in the building along with the clothiers.

An early advertisement for prominent real estate magnet, J.J. Fairbanks.

In later years, the building would be occupied and owned by Kohfeldt and Sons Realty, a well-known and long-established firm in Denison that lasted for decades. The firm maintained the original character of the building throughout their time at the location, leaving Denison with one of its most intact commercial structures from the 1800's.

An advertisement placed to welcome Johns-Manville to the area, placed by Kohfeldt and Son.

The building was sold in the 1990's and went through several owners until it was purchased by Bill and Cindy Pratt in 2016. The couple remodeled the interior of the building while preserving the incredible exterior and leased the second-floor loft as an apartment with the main floor going to Vitina's Deli.

When workers were doing cleanup and repair of the basement, they began to feel uneasy and a chill went through the air. Quickly, one of the workers turned around and snapped a picture, convinced someone was in the room with them.

The result of the picture was something beyond belief. There was indeed a figure in the room, and it appeared in the photo. Upon close inspection, there appears to be the figure of a woman wearing an evening gown looking almost directly at the camera. This is one of the incredibly rare photos of a ghost in the Denison area and we were able to include it in this book below.

Current loft residents, Matt and Melanie Truxal have also reported strange happenings. The young couple has heard their Amazon Alexa speaking to someone, as if a request has been made. However, upon reviewing requests made to the Alexa, none can be found. They have also had experiences with a smoke detector going off but stopping soon after they asked the spirit to leave them alone.

Other strange occurrences for the young loft-dwellers include strange noises heard throughout the loft, and sensations of cold chills in different parts of the loft that are felt when the residents walk around. They seem to occur more prominently at night, and for some reason seem to happen more to the Matt than to Melanie.

This eerie image from the basement of 118 West Main is one of the few photos ever captured of a Denison spirit.

Popular opinion is that the building is haunted by the ghost of Maude Kramer, the young woman who lost her life during Denison's Night of Terror. The building at 118 backs up to the alley of what used to be known as Skiddy Street, a popular location for brothels and saloons in Denison's early days.

The fact that the occurrences in the building tend to happen more to men might indicate that the spirit is indeed that of a woman. Is Maude trying to reach out, in the hopes that a man would be able to help her? Or is it for another reason? Her life was ended by a man, perhaps she is trying to haunt those men who come too close to the area of her death?

A Curious Graveyard

The following article appeared in the *Dallas Morning News* on May 3, 1891. While no haunting correlates with the article, the existence of such a macabre graveyard in Denison's historic downtown is enough to spurn nightmares.

"Denison-Denison has a most peculiar graveyard. In fact, it is probable that not another cemetery of the kind is to be found in the state. The burial ground is a small (piece) of land lying north and immediately adjoining the Missouri, Kansas and Texas freight depot, and is used for the interment of hands, legs, fingers and such other parts of human beings as are mashed or mutilated by the cars in such a manner as necessitate amputation.

In the MK&T yards in this city and among its hundreds of miles of track north, south, and west of the city accidents are frequently occurring, and a large number of those injured are forwarded here for medical and surgical treatment.

The freight building is used for such purposes, and the vacant lot north of the platform is used as a depository for amputated substance. Two weeks ago the legs of little Johnny Wells were interred in this peculiar graveyard, and this morning the right foot of E.R. McCain found a grave at the same place."

The area between the current depot building and the Main Street Lumber annex building is where the appendage graveyard can be found.

Birds Eye View from 1883 showing the location of the freight depot at center right.

The site is driven past by countless vehicles each day with few passengers and drivers realizing they are so close to such a ghastly resting place. The next time you drive along East Main Street take a moment to reflect on all of those body parts buried not far from the road.

Chapter
Four

Frontier Village
The Oldest Homes & Spirits in the County

On the western edge of Denison there sits a village composed of the oldest homes in Grayson County. This old-time village is nestled on 14 acres alongside Loy Lake Park and has been described as a peaceful place for both living and spiritual beings.

Frontier Village got its start in 1966 when a group of concerned citizens, led by Otto Vehle, attended a meeting of the Sherman Chamber of Commerce concerning the fate of Sherman's oldest house, the Nettie Bass home, at 215 West Houston. The property the house sat on was purchased for a downtown parking lot during the urban renewal craze that swept the nation from the 1950's through the 1970's.

Many people wanted to see the home preserved for future generations; however, the Chamber board members rejected the idea. Vehle and his crew did not give up hope and contacted the Old Settlers Park Association on Grand Avenue in Sherman to see about possibly moving the house to that location. In January of 1967, the group voted to incorporate under the name of Old Settlers Village of Grayson County and Vehle was named coordinator over events.

On August 18, 1967, plans were made to move the Bass house to Loy Park, where Old Settlers Village of Grayson Count planned to construct a typical frontier village reflecting life in the mid-1800's.

Ground was broken on September 9, 1967, and a 99-year lease of 17 acres was negotiated with the Grayson County Commissioners Court (the owners of Loy Lake) for $1. The commissioners graciously paid $2,775 to have a chain link fence built around 14 acres in November of 1973, to help with vandalism to the site. In 1977, the name was officially changed to Grayson County Frontier Village.

Several of the homes throughout the Village are said to be haunted, with strange occurrences happening to both staff and visitors alike. The main one that will be focused on in the book is a small, non-descript, cabin that seems somewhat unassuming compared to those surrounding it. Yet this building has one of the most unique histories of any building in Grayson County.

The Mistress of Glen Eden

Grayson County once boasted a plantation full of glamour, hardships, violence, and romance of the frontier country. The plantation home was built by Colonel Holland Coffee in 1843 for his young wife, Sophia, whom he married in 1837.

The palatial residence, named Glen Eden, was located along the banks of the Red River near Preston Bend and was the capital of Southern hospitality and gentility throughout the pioneer era.

Colonel Coffee operated a trading outpost to supply intrepid pioneers and to trade trinkets and provisions to the Indians in exchange for the release of white prisoners. In one instance, Holland traded 400 yards of calico and a large number of blankets and beads in exchange for a captive woman and her two children. The outpost was located along the trail that most Forty-Niners used as they headed West in search of gold, and was the first road designated by the Republic of Texas, named the Preston Road.

In 1840, a company of Texas Rangers were sent to augment protecting of the post, which was the "jumping off place" into the uncharted frontier. Commanding the Ranger force was Capt. William Preston, whose name was used for the naming of the community. With an inn, stores, the Rangers' stockade and the first Methodist Church in Texas, Preston was the largest community in North Texas in the early half of the 19th century, and also the head of Red River navigation. If Glen Eden's history were to be told through the eyes of one of its inhabitants, it would have to be those of Sophia, Col. Coffee's wife.

Sophia was born in Fort Wayne, Indiana and eloped with a German schoolteacher, Jesse Aughinbaugh, at the age of 16. The officer brought her to Texas where, through circumstances unknown, he deserted her. No mention of him ever appeared in any of her writings or in any histories of her life.

Sophia's life following her supposed desertion is hard to follow but does add to the legend and mystery that surrounds her. She claimed to have been the first woman on the field following the Battle of San Jacinto and insisted she nursed an injured Sam Houston, thus beginning a lifelong friendship.

Colonel Coffee met Sophia sometime in 1837, and they set up housekeeping in a shanty at Preston, surrounded by a stockade for protection from marauders. They would live in this home for five years with their closest neighbor being 25 miles away.

Prosperity followed for the couple with massive land acquisitions and growth from the trading post. The home that would come to be known as Glen Eden was started in 1843 and was originally a two-story oak home with a pitched roof and separate kitchen. The forty-eight foot long, foundation was made of native stone and supported the four-room structure. Eventually, the home was expanded and siding from Jefferson was added coupled with long porches on either side of the ever-expanding home.

Glen Eden as it appeared before Lake Texoma was formed.

A kitchen and wine cellar, along with a new roof rounded out the additions and improvements. Sophia loved plants and had rock gardens and a brick greenhouse constructed so she could cultivate year-around. The plantation home also boasted vast amounts of orchards and vineyards.

Catalpas that grew about the grounds for many years had their start from seed brought from California by General Albert Sidney Johnson as a gift for Sophia. Subsequently, all catalpa trees in our area are descendants from Sophia's trees.

Other guests who honored the house were General Robert E. Lee, General U.S. Grant and General Fitzhugh Lee. Legend has it that General Sam Houston stayed at Glen Eden during a visit to Grayson to speak at a celebration for the naming of Sherman as the county seat. A giant magnolia tree that graced the lawn of Glen Eden was reportedly a gift from Houston to the Coffees.

The mistress of Glen Eden, Sophia, later in life.

Although a wonderful place, Glen Eden was not without its tragedies. Colonel Coffee was stabbed to death at his trading post in 1846. He left Sophia with over 5,000 acres of land, nineteen slaves, herds of horses and cattle, and his trading post business. Sophia's second husband, Major Butts, was killed by William Quantrill's men near Sherman during the Civil War.

Later in the winter, after her husband's death, Sophia would pull off a feat that would make her famous in the South for years to come. Yankee soldiers arrived at Glen Eden searching for Confederate troops that were known to be in the area.

Sophia gladly welcomed the soldiers into her home, offering them a home-cooked meal and the keys to the wine cellar.

Once all of the soldiers had become sufficiently drunk, Sophia locked the cellar door and rode all the way to Fort Warren to warn the Confederate soldiers. The Yankees never knew she was gone and were never able to find the Confederate soldiers that they searched for. This act of valor earned Sophia the title of "the Confederate Paul Revere."

After the war, Sophia became the wife of Judge James Porter of Waco and returned with him to Glen Eden. Judge Porter died in 1886 after a prolonged illness and was followed by 82-year-old Sophia on August 27, 1897. Sophia Suttonfield Aughinbaugh Coffee Butts Porter was buried beside her last husband in the Preston Cemetery following an elaborate funeral procession led by four black horses decorated with black net coats.

The plantation would pass through several owners following the death of Sophia before its fate would ultimately be decided by the ever-increasing movement of progress. The construction of the Denison Dam spelt doom for the famous plantation, as the home and surrounding land were to be inundated following the damming of the Red River. Local historian, Judge Bryant, had the house dismantled with the idea of reconstructing the home at another site for use as a museum.

Sophia's headstone after it was relocated to Pottsboro due to the rising waters of Lake Texoma.

However, Corps of Engineer officers in charge of building the dam mistook the large piles of the dismantled home for firewood and burned much of it in huge bonfires to help keep workers warm. Local history advocate, Nellie Chambers salvaged what she could and had the logs reconstructed into smaller cabins that are now among the historic structures at Frontier Village.

Very little is left to show the fame and fortune of one of the most amazing women to have lived in North Texas. The logs salvaged from her burned home are one of the direct ties to Sophia herself. Volunteers at the Village claim that Sophia's spirit remains amongst the ruins of her once-grand Glen Eden.

Within one of the cabins salvaged from the ruins there sits a small dish of pearls. Volunteers will stage the room and drape the pearls slightly out of the bowl so they will be visible to museum attendees. No matter who arranges the pearls outside of the bowl, they are always placed neatly back inside when volunteers go to check on the cabin.

Others have seen the figure of a woman walking through the cabin, yet no one is inside when the building is inspected. The woman is wearing a fine evening gown and will sometimes look directly at onlookers as she glides by. Could Sophia still be holding onto her life as Mistress of Glen Eden? Is it possible that she finds comfort amongst the ruins of her beloved plantation?

Chapter Five

Waples-Platter Grocery Company
The Ever-Watchful Night Guard

The Waples-Platter Grocery Company is one of the few companies founded before the city of Denison came into existence. The company began in 1871 as a commissary that served the M, K, &T railroad workers as they extended the rail line into Texas.

The commissary was located in a tent at Chickasaw Ben Colbert's Ferry along the Red River where it was suspected the MKT Railroad would be coming through and was begun by Sam Hanna and Joe Owens.

Samuel McAfee Hanna Sr. (August 8, 1834- November 21, 1903) was born in Shelby County Kentucky and made his way towards Texas and the Wild West frontier in the 1870's. Little is known about Joe Owens. The commissary was stocked with bags of coffee beans, a cracker barrel, bulk sugar, and barrels of lard, and was housed in a tent for six to seven months to provide hunters and ranchers with food as well as much-needed ammunition.

Once the fledgling city of Denison had been plotted and lots sold in September of 1872, the two enterprising men moved their firm known as Hanna, Owens & Co. four miles to the south and became the first wholesale grocery company to arrive in the newly formed city. The firm set up shop in a 25 ft. by 80 ft. building directly across the street from the railroad depot in the 100 block of East Main in 1873.

The primitive operation included the handling of buffalo hides brought in by hunters from the prairies and the shipment of provisions by ox team into Indian Territory and other surrounding areas. Freighters would commonly haul hides from Fort Griffin to Denison and return with supplies for cattle ranchers, hunters, and merchants.

Andrew Fox (A.F.) Platter (August 17, 1850- December 24, 1932), a dry goods clerk in Missouri, came to Denison in 1877 to visit his sister and was thoroughly impressed by the potential of the frontier town. He returned in 1878 to become a bookkeeper for Hanna and Owens, and bought Owens' interest in 1882. With Platter's purchase, the firm became known as Hanna, Platter & Co. with the name quickly changing to Hanna, Platter & Lingo with the addition of Edward Henry (E.H.) Lingo (October 11, 1838-January 27, 1927) to the partnership in the same year.

In 1883, A.F. Platter married a woman by the name of Fannie Waples (August 18, 1857- December 13, 1947) and together they encouraged her father E.B. Waples and her brothers, Paul and John, to buy major interests in the business. Several years later the company went through yet another name change, as it became Hanna, Platter & Waples when Edward Bridell (E.B.) Waples (October 25, 1814-October 4, 1898) bought an interest in the company in 1885.

E.B. Waples was also named president of the firm in 1885 and became very active in the city; the Waples Memorial United Methodist Church in Denison bears his name for his contributions to the church. This same year, 1885, a large elegant warehouse and headquarter building was constructed at 104 E. Main in Denison.

The new warehouse and headquarters was an architectural marvel designed by architect P. Lelardoux of Muskogee, Ok, and was a two-story structure with cast iron pilasters in the façade, terracotta lions head statues, keystones and segmented arch openings. The building was meant to symbolize the company's prominence in Denison, and the large brick edifice did just that for 128 years before it was demolished in 2013.

The company's line of grocery products known as the White Swan line was introduced in 1886 to symbolize the company's quality in packaging. The white swan floating on pure water was an image chosen to represent the high standards that Waples-Platter required of their food products.

Waples-Platter Grocery Company ca 1890.

Shortly afterward in 1887 Sam Hanna sold his interest in the company to the sons of Waples, Paul (February 4, 1850-November 16, 1916) and John Waples (April 28, 1848- January 3, 1912) and the firm became known as Waples-Platter & Company.

In 1891, the company was officially incorporated as Waples-Platter Grocer Company and Paul Waples succeeded his father as president before the end of the year. Paul would eventually move to Fort Worth with the company, where in 1906 he became the founder of the Fort Worth Star that would later become the famed Fort Worth Star-Telegram.

With the success of the company came the need for growth and expansion, which occurred with the opening of the first branch house at Gainesville in 1890 and the establishment of the company at Fort Worth in 1893.

Fort Worth would play a crucial role in the company's development eventually becoming the site of the Waples-Platter headquarters. In 1897, the firm's Wapco brand was originated, and branches were opened at Bowie and Dublin. In 1898, the Concho line was added, giving the company its third private label.

The year 1902 saw the beginning of operations in Dallas with 1905 bringing branch houses at Greenville and Ada, Oklahoma. In 1907, the Federal Food and Drug Act became effective, but no re-adjustment of company standards was necessary due to the high-quality policies already practiced by Waples-Platter.

The company also came into the manufacturing business beginning in 1906 with the construction of a coffee roasting plant inside an historic structure at 110-112 S. Houston Ave. in Denison. The "Roasting Ovens" at the plant were eight-foot cylinders, which the employees fired by hand with coke.

The coffee roasting plant was followed shortly afterwards with a food processing division at Fort Worth in 1913. The year 1913 also marked the birth of the Waples-Platter Canning Plant, later known as Ranch Style, Inc.

In 1914 Waples-Platter purchased Blanke & Co., a coffee and tea company based out of Dallas, and began roasting coffee there, whilst simultaneously continuing operations at the

Denison plant. The year 1915 marked the beginning of the company's label printing division.

Photo showing 110-112 S. Houston at extreme right.

Paul Waples died in 1916 and his brother-in-law, A.F. Platter, became president of the company. In 1917, the container manufacturing section or "box factory" was begun at Fort Worth in a 40 by 75-foot frame building. Ten employees made packing cases for the nearby food processing plant and boxes for the Denison and Dallas coffee roasting plants. The last action of the company before the roaring twenties began was the opening of a branch house at Clovis, New Mexico in 1919.

In 1982, White Swan Inc. and four other subsidiaries were sold to Fleming companies of Oklahoma City for $91 million. In 1983, the Fort Worth owners sold Great Western Foods-Ranch Style to American Home Products Corp., the New-York based maker of Anacin, Chef Boy-Ar-Dee and hundreds of other consumer products.

In 1985, White Swan purchased the M&M Harlingen Company of Corpus Christi. July of 1988 was a big month when White Swan purchased William E. Davis of Oklahoma City and Standard Food Service of West Virginia. The managers of White Swan then teamed up with outside investors to purchase the company from Fleming to end the year as the largest privately owned food service company in the United States.

In 1991, the Watson Food Service Industries was added to the White Swan family and in 1992; the addition of Restaurant Food Supply of Columbus Ohio and Mom's Produce of Dallas made the company even larger. Through various purchases, the White Swan name is no longer in existence as it once was, but it is safe to say that company, along with the men who worked so hard to build it, will forever have a place in the history of Texas.

Waples-Platter Grocery Company, ca. 1930's

The building was patrolled by an employee who walked the premises each night, both inside the building and around the outer perimeter. Ann Paulson, long-time business owner at the site, claimed that on many occasions footsteps could be heard inside the building even when she was the only one there.

Because of the way the building was constructed, footsteps on the outside are also very audible from the interior. She claimed there would be slow, methodical footsteps pacing around the building at night, but upon further inspection, no one could ever be found even remotely close to the building.

The author worked at the site for several years and would often have to go to the large second floor that was used for storage. The giant space held some of the oldest items from Denison's history, as the building owner's grandfather, Pat Tobin, drove the first train into Denison from the north. While no steps were heard, there was always a feeling of being watched, as if the guard never really relinquished his duties, even after death.

Chapter Six

Denison's Black Tuesday
The Worst Disaster the City has ever Known

On November 21, 1944, one of Denison's worst disasters in the city's history took place. A simple fender bender turned into a fiery holocaust that engulfed an entire city-block radius surrounding the accident scene.

Two days before Thanksgiving, at around 5:00 pm, a Dodge sedan rear-ended a butane gas truck at the intersection of Morton Street and Maurice Avenue. The sedan was occupied by Mr. and Mrs. John Marshall, Mrs. Otto C. Ahlers of Sherman, and Mrs. R.B. Marshall of Dallas, who were returning to Sherman after visiting a relative in Durant, Oklahoma.

The butane truck was driven by a local man, Jeff Whitfield. All seemed normal, until Whitfield noticed that the crash had caused a broken drain in the truck that regulated the pressure, causing vapor to spew out of the broken pipe. Once the driver realized what was happening, he yelled a warning for everyone in the area to run for cover. Like most modern accidents, a large crowd had gathered to investigate what had happened.

Whitfield was joined by Earl Vick, an employee of the Fisher Grocery Store at 1431 W. Morton. Vick tried to urge his store patrons to flee the scene as he ran from the store and down the street. While some heeded the warning, it was simply too late for most. Within two minutes of the accident, the entire area was engulfed in flames that claimed the lives of thirteen individuals.

Vick would later state that he ran from the store, urging people to follow him to escape the possible blast. He ran east along Morton and could feel the heat on his back when he heard the blast. He threw himself to the ground and claimed the "earth rocked from the concussion".

Along with the driver and passengers in the sedan, three others lost their lives trying to flee from Fisher Grocery seconds before the blast rocked the neighborhood. One man, F.L. Nix left the store and ran to a small warehouse east of the grocery store where he later lost his life.

The newspaper reported that a thick, white vapor spread across the block and settled to the ground since butane is heavier than air. An errant spark ignited the butane that had spread among the crowd and surrounding buildings, causing a chain of three major explosions.

A nighboring store near the blast site of Denison's Black Tuesday.

A nearby warehouse was completely demolished, and a newly painted house and garage apartment were stripped down to bare wood. Seven other buildings also caught fire and were burning profusely when firefighters arrived at the scene.

The damage from the blast occurred in a random order. Plate glass windows in the nearby Fisher Grocery were not damaged, yet a horse in a barn a block away was blown through the wall by the blast and ended up several houses down from its original location. The explosion was so intense that clothing from the victims had been burned and blown from their bodies, leaving an eerie scene of clothing strewn around the scene of the accident.

All of the paint was stripped from a nearby home.

According to Fire Chief Pat Lowe, five different water lines were laid to handle the inferno and all available fire and rescue equipment was diverted to the scene.

The explosion was so huge and so catastrophic that Perrin Air Force Base sent military policemen, along with ambulance and medical personnel to aid the survivors. The scene was so dismal and chaotic, that Sherman also sent all available ambulances to help carry injured to local hospitals.

Seven people died the first night at the Katy Hospital, and six others passed away during the days following the explosion. The last to die was 12-year-old Lonnie Jo Hammons, who had been sent to the grocery store by his mother for a can of tomatoes.

While the area looks much different today and many of the buildings have been replaced by more modern structures, it is still easy to imagine the scene that scarred the area for so many years.

Locals claim to see figures running from the area, as if trying to escape some horrible event. Others have witnessed strange sightings of people walking around shell-shocked, as if they do not know where to go or where they are. These people are described as wearing clothes that do not fit our place and time, could these mysterious figures be the victims of that fateful day?

Chapter Seven

The Madonna Hospital
A Place of Healing and Hauntings

For many years in Denison's early history, the city was without a formal hospital. To help alleviate this situation, the citizens passed a bond in 1913 allowing for a special tax to be assessed for the construction of a new hospital at 411 East Hull Street. Construction began on February 12, 1913 and would continue for much of that year. Although the hospital was built and was a shining example of civic pride, it was not without its problems.

The original idea for the hospital was that Denison would construct the building and the Katy Railroad would lease the space. Railroad officials turned down the proposition stating that they were not financially able to take on the responsibility of a city hospital at that time.

All seemed lost for a short time until Dr. J.G. Ellis and his two doctor sons took over operations in 1914, hoping to bring new energy to the hospital and surrounding community. However, their venture was ultimately unsuccessful, and the doctors began to look for a new owner.

Denison's City Hospital shortly after completion at 411 East Hull Street.

By 1919, local papers were calling the hospital the "white elephant" of Denison. It was at this time that an attempt was made to have some type of religious denomination take over operations of the hospital.

The hospital would pass through varying states of success and failure until the Sisters of Divine Providence, a Catholic sisterhood based in San Antonio, took over the property in 1943. Under the new ownership agreement, the facility was to be completely remodeled by the Sisters with up-to-date furnishings and equipment in exchange for the deed to the property.

The Madonna Hospital officially opened its doors on September 1, 1945, and was hailed as one of the finest medical institutions in the state. The Sisters were housed in a convent in the east wing of the building and offered a chapel on the main floor for patients and visitors.

The ground floor was home to St. Joseph Hall where lab, x-ray facilities, drug room, laundry room, blood bank, and emergency room were all located. The administrative offices were located on the second floor, while the third floor, known as Madonna Hall, contained the maternity ward and a surgery suite known as St. Ann Hall.

Madonna Hospital after expansion and renovations.

By the mid-1950's, the hospital was suffering from growing pains and a new wing was added to the back of the hospital building, nearly doubling the size of the facility.

In the 1960's the small hospital was no longer able to keep up with the high demand of patients. In order to meet the needs of residents, a new facility was constructed in 1965 near the old Katy Hospital on Memorial Drive and opened as Denison's Memorial Hospital. Nearly 10 years later, the hospital would be renamed Texoma Medical Center and would serve for decades before being replaced by a new structure on Highway 75.

In 1975, the old Madonna Hospital was acquired for the Denison Hospital Authority and renamed Texoma Medical Center East. The facility operated as a 36-bed psychiatric unit before becoming a nursing home for a time.

Madonna Hospital shortly before being demolished.

Following the closing of the nursing home, the old hospital went through a series of owners with many plans that never came to fruition. The Madonna structure was vacant and decaying for a number of years before being demolished in 2016 to make way for future residential development.

While it sat vacant, local neighbors often saw the figures of men and women through some of the broken windows. The figures were described as wearing hospital gowns, with some also having surgical masks on. Noises coming from within the building were also a common occurrence with several residents hearing blood-curdling screams that would often set the neighborhood on edge.

While the building was demolished, is it possible that the spirits from within the old hospital can still be found around its site? Only time will tell...

Chapter Eight

The Fairbanks House
The House Down the Hill

One of Denison's largest homes was once located on the busy section of Old Highway 75 just south of downtown, with a once-exclusive address of 1801 South Austin Avenue.

The opulent home was built in 1890 by local real estate tycoon, J.J. Fairbanks. There, on what used to be mostly undeveloped wilderness, he housed his prized racing horses on a 640-acre tract of land surrounding the home.

John Joseph (J.J.) Fairbanks was a mere 17 years old when he moved from various places including Bloomfield, N.J., Brooklyn, N.Y., and Meriden, Conn. After a time, he moved to Kansas and founded the town of Colony in Anderson County.

From there he moved to Denison to serve as paymaster for the MK&T Railroad. It was also said that he founded the town of Fairbanks in Harris County in 1895, but never lived there.

The Fairbanks house ca. 1900.

Fairbanks' wife, Edith Kirk, was born in Mountain View, N.J. on January 1, 1840. She married J.J. on January 1, 1867 in Kokomo, Indiana. Edith was from an incredibly wealthy family, and it was her money that enabled the couple to build such a lavish home.

The house featured four fireplaces, 12-foot ceilings, 10-foot stained-glass doors and numerous stained-glass windows throughout the rooms. Fairbanks traveled far and wide, including New York, to buy furnishings and décor for his new mansion. The wood used within the home was shipped from various points across the country, making the home one of the most diverse in Denison.

Each room in the home was built with a different species of wood including mahogany, pecan, cherry, and tiger oak, now extinct to Texas. The wood on the 200-pound pocket doors corresponds to the room with some doors featuring cherry on one side and tiger oak on the other.

Another unique feature of the hilltop home was the addition of a catwalk along the top of the home. Local lore says that J.J. had this installed so he could enjoy his gambling pursuits with his friends. A lookout would sit along the catwalk and call down if the law, or worse the wives, started toward the home. The catwalk also allowed for panoramic views of the surrounding countryside and glimpses of downtown Denison.

Three children would be born to the intrepid couple; Kirk, May, and Lolita Maud. Not long after the home was completed, J.J. and Edith were divorced, and Edith moved to Kansas where she became a very successful real estate investor. Fairbanks would go on to marry a hugely successful local real estate woman by the name of Eliza Williams in 1910, and spent the rest of his life in the home until 1922.

Eventually, Eliza Fairbanks sold the home to S.W. Bergen, then it was sold to Mr. And Mrs. Clarence A. Kennedy in 1930. Prior to the Kennedy's, the home had been lit by gaslights. They added electricity and refinished many of the hardwood floors throughout the home. By this time, the once grand estate had been pared down to 13 ½ acres. Much of the original property was divided up into lots for construction of individual homes.

The Kimberly's raised goats and sheep on the property as well as grapes, watermelon, cantaloupe, and a variety of other crops. They were well known for their grapes, which were said to be some of the best in the county. The property bordered the early day property of T.V. Munson, noted horticulturist, who grew grapes in large multitudes. It was thought that some of these grapes were what grew on the Kennedy property.

Mr. Kimberly died just a few years after purchasing the home and Mrs. Kimberly kept it for several years. She rented the house out for a time when she went to live with her daughter in Houston. She died in 1972 and the house was listed for sale by her daughter, Mrs. Crabb.

It was during this period between listing and sale that the house was virtually abandoned, and vandals soon struck the once-palatial estate. The chandeliers were destroyed, and ceramic tiles were pulled from two of the four fireplaces, smashing the mirrors above them in the process.

The original gaslights on the front porch disappeared along with an historic fireplace front from one of the downstairs living rooms. Vandals even stole the doors to a corner cabinet from the kitchen.

Although the home lost many of the grand fixtures, it still retained quite a bit of its historic character. The hand carved solid wood staircase and woodwork throughout the home were proof of the once elegant interior. Gingerbread trim on the outside and a cornerstone inscribed 1890 helped to further date the house.

Harold Haddock, a car dealer in Denison, purchased the home and five acres fronting the highway in the fall of 1978. Initially, he planned to tear down the structure in order to build a new car lot. However, his wife, Jane, had other plans that called for the preservation of one of Denison's landmarks. The only way the plan could work though, was if the house was moved to a different site.

A house mover, Ruel Golden, from Coalgate, Oklahoma made contact with Haddock's and said he could move the home, but because of the size of the three-story mansion, it would only be moved to another location on the adjoining property. Because of the way the 5-acre tract was laid out, the house could be moved to the back of the lot and turned slightly to face South rather than East, like it had for the previous 89 years.

With an estimated weight of 250,000 pounds, simply moving the house was no small task. By relocating the house directly down the hill to the south, all three stories could remain intact. Any moves to other locations would have necessitated the house being chopped up into small pieces and then reassembled at a new site.

Fireplaces and chimneys were demolished in the home and the large stones that served as the foundation for the home were removed and marked so they could be replaced after the move. When the fireplaces were removed, many of the bricks dissolved and could not be used in the future.

The abandoned Fairbanks home during the 1960's.

Inch by inch, the home was moved nearly 200 yards downhill with the help of two seven-ton trucks. The procession was halted three separate times to remove limbs from the path. Nervous gasps were let out by the crowd each time one of the trucks groaned under the weight of the massive structure, and huge cheers arose when the house safely reached its destination at the bottom of the hill.

The new address for the home was 200 Prospect Lane in a secluded lot behind the car dealership. The Haddock's had every intention of restoring the home, but that dream never came to fruition after the structure was stabilized and the foundation reconstructed.

Jean and Larry Lonis purchased the home in the early 1980's with the intention of returning the home to its original splendor. When they first moved in, the house was in complete disarray with no hot water, only single bulb light fixtures hanging in each room and no drawers or doors on the kitchen cabinets.

The couple quickly got to work researching the style of the homes and were able to restore it completely after a year of hard work and determination.

An article was published in a local newspaper featuring the restoration of the home and stated the following:

"The inviting entryway where its solid oak banisters and trim lead upstairs to a white plush carpeted hallway have been refinished to its original beauty. Peacock wallpaper reaches from the stairway to the second floor ceiling in strips that measure as much as 245 inches. Lonis had to build a scaffold to hang the paper in this area. He said it took longer to build the scaffold than it did to hang the paper.

Every room in the house except a back hallway has wallpaper of the 1890 period, and all oak and cherry wood woodwork and floors have been restored to their original beauty.

Jean made every curtain and drape in the house using literally hundreds of yards of fabric patterned after the 1890's era. She went to far as to be generous in the length of their drapes, carrying out the thought of the 1890's that drapes that were too long showed the owners could afford to be extravagant."

The lavish interior of the Fairbanks home. Note the intricae woodwork on the staircase.

The couple lived in the home for several years before selling to Walter and Lynn Marrable in 2008. The Marrables did some updating of the home and created the Molly Cherry Bed & Breakfast.

The B&B was quite successful and remained in business until it was sold after a few years of operation. The home and surrounding property is now privately owned.

There were reports of the house being haunted while it sat vacant, but they don't go into a lot of detail. Some say they could see the figure of Mr. Fairbanks walking the catwalk of the home and loud noises could be heard by passersby.

The Fairbanks home as it appears today.

The noises and figures are said to have stopped after the home was moved. Could J.J. have been guarding his vacant property against demolition? Was his spirit able to rest only after knowing the house would be saved for future generations?

Chapter Nine

Woodlake
Denison's Lost Paradise

Nearly right in between Sherman and Denison lies a lake and surrounding area that once was the social hub for the twin cities. It all began in the late 1800's when the only transportation around Sherman and Denison was mule drawn trolleys.

J.P. Crearer, a Canadian, moved to the area in 1896 and purchased the mule-drawn Denison-Sherman Trolley Line with the intention of putting in an Electric Rail System between the two cities.

The project took nearly five years of development and planning, and one major need of the fledgling enterprise was water to power the electric line. Crearer chose Tanyard Springs, about halfway between Denison and Sherman, where there was a natural spring used by early-day Indians to tan hides.

Crearer and his crew drilled a 900-foot well and built a powerhouse and railway station on the north end of the lake he created by damming up the spring. Once completed, he changed the name from Tanyard Springs to Woodlake, named for the vast woodlands surrounding the picturesque lake, and the area has been known as such ever since.

The lake and park opened to great fanfare on May 1901 with the new, electric, Denison & Sherman Transit Company providing free rides from both cities. The event was a huge success and thus began the golden years of travel via the Interurban line.

Woodlake during its heyday.

The lakeside resort was said to have been one of the most beautiful sights imaginable. Not only were the lake waters clear because it was spring fed, but it was also surrounded by flowering gardens including roses, crepe myrtles, and magnolias with profuse blooms during the summer months.

Woodlake expanded to include a zoo, boat rides, a large slide capable of handling canoes, as well as an opera house. Each boat was rented for 25 cents an hour and had a number painted on its side. Once the hour was up, a bell would be rung for all to hear, and a signal would be held up signaling which boat was to return to the pier.

Some of the animals in the zoo included Chinese peacocks, deer, goats, donkeys, and even a small black bear cub. The most impressive animals, however, were the South American spider monkeys, well known for stealing resort patrons' jewelry and hair ribbons whenever someone strayed too near the monkey cage.

In 1915, an opera house, called The Casino, was erected and a wooden pool known as "The Pig Pen" was completed. The pool was put along the east side of the lake and featured wooden walls as well as a wooden floor that grew copious amounts of algae over the years.

The Casino was a two-story Victorian style building that housed a plush entrance lobby, a coin operated Victrola, and an imported player piano that played popular tunes of the era. It also featured an auditorium with a seating capacity of 900, and the capability of being used for motion pictures during the summer months.

With the advent of the motor vehicle, crowds began to dwindle at Woodlake. Several serious accidents, including a handful of fatalities, occurred along the electric railway near Woodlake, further deterring people from using that form of travel.

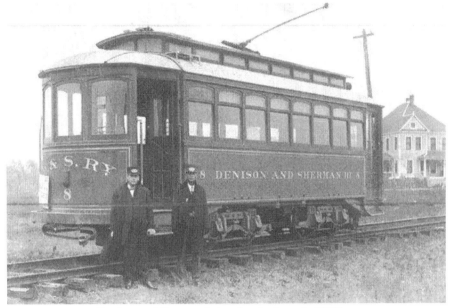

Denison and Sherman Interurban in the early 1920's.

By 1929, the lake, amusement park, and grounds had been purchased by private citizens. An agreement was reached with the North Texas Baptists for the site to host a two-week camp each summer for 50 years. An open-air tabernacle, cafeteria, and several small buildings were constructed during this era.

Steps leading to the Casino are still visible as are the rock paths and main office foundation across the lake. The spillway is the only other original landmark remaining other than the dance hall that was screened in for dormitory use. The interurban depot and powerhouse stand in silent ruin and various brick paths still meander around the lake.

Steps lead into the lake at Woodlake Park, ca. 2007

There have long been stories of hauntings at the lakeside resort. Nearby property owners say they can hear classical Victorian tunes coming from the area surrounding the lake at night, and it's not uncommon to see ghostly lights coming from the area where the old depot and pavilion once stood.

These sightings lead locals to believe that some of the park-goers never left, and instead chose to live out their spiritual days in what has become the lost paradise of North Texas.

Chapter Ten

Denison's Night of Terror
The City's first Serial Killer

The night of May 17 and early morning of May 18, 1892, have gone down in Denison's history as its night of terror. That fateful night saw four innocent women shot, with three of them dying from their wounds. The young city was rocked by the events of this night, causing history to take note of Denison's most terrifying night on record.

The first victim was the beautiful Mrs. Hattie G. Haynes, only 28 years old at the time. She lived in Southwest Denison in the neighborhood where Woodlawn Boulevard and Bullock Street intersect. This area was known as The Boulevards and was an up-and-coming neighborhood for the city's wealthy and elite.

The homes of The Boulevards addition were grand, and the lots were large, with the Haynes' home being built for an estimated $6,000, a small fortune at that time. The Haynes grand home was located close to that of her parents, Dr. and Mrs. J.D. Garner, near the impressive Exposition Hall grounds.

A drawing of the Exposition Hall from 1891.

Mrs. Haynes, along with her mother, and her husband, Dr. J. H. Haynes, had traveled into town to join various festivities that were taking place that evening.

Dr. Haynes attended a meeting to organize the new Elks' Lodge above the State National Bank on Main Street. Meanwhile, Mrs. Haynes and her mother were at the First Methodist Episcopal Church, North, on the northwest corner of Fannin Avenue and Woodard Street to see a literary program followed by a social on the church lawn.

The First Methodist Episcopal Church, North ca.1900. One of the last places Hattie Haynes was seen alive.

Shortly after 10 pm, Mrs. Haynes and her mother rode the "dummy" line, a steam train that operated along Woodard Street, out to the Cotton Mill and Exposition Building into the neighborhood of their homes. A large field separated the home of the Haynes and that of her mother and father, the Garners.

As the two women approached the Haynes residence, Mrs. Haynes saw that a lamp was lit in the house. She stated, "You need not go in with me, I see the doctor is already here, as a light is burning. We put them all out when we left." At that, they said goodnight. It would be the last time Mrs. Garner would ever see her daughter alive. A few minutes later, Garner heard her daughter's frantic screams.

The Garners rushed to the Hayes home and searched each room but could find no sign of their daughter. Two lamps were burning, one in the lower floor and another one in the second story. The entire house was in shambles with debris strewn about the rooms as if some great struggle had taken place.

Shortly thereafter, three shots were fired nearby, causing Dr. Garner to run from the house and search, but he could not tell from which directions the shots had come. The frenzied couple stopped their search momentarily so they could wire the sheriff for help.

A man by the name of Houston Bostwick had ridden the motor car home with the women and had heard what had happened. He rushed back onto the line and ran to the Elks' Hall to tell Dr. Haynes the news of his wife's disappearance and relay that a search was currently underway. The entire lodge shut down and all members volunteered their service to help find the fair and much-loved Mrs. Haynes.

Sheriff Lee McAfee arrived from Sherman with his bloodhounds to help aid in the search. The night was very dark and the woods so dense as to be almost impenetrable. Dozens of lamps and lanterns glittered amongst the trees and underbrush as friends and family tried valiantly to find their friend.

Two hours after the shooting, W.W. Bostwick found the body of Mrs. Haynes in a thicket 100 yards from the Haynes house. Diamond earrings had been violently removed from her ears and diamond rings had been stripped from her fingers with a knife, causing severe disfigurements of her beautiful hands. She had been wounded by a shot to her breast and was then killed when a ball from a 44-caliber revolver bullet passed through her brain before burying itself in the ground. The death was an execution and rocked the neighborhood.

It was surmised that Mrs. Haynes had interrupted a burglary in her home, thus catching the robber in the act. Fearing she would be able to identify him, he killed Mrs. Haynes when she tried to escape towards her parents' house by cutting across the field.

News of the terrible death quickly reached fellow citizens and intensified the excitement and fear felt throughout the city. This was not to be the only tragedy of the night. While all of this was happening, more shootings were underway in the fledgling Gate City that would have a resounding impact for years to come.

There was a businessman named Tom who operated a restaurant on Austin Avenue and was known to be of ill repute. His place of business had a reputation as a business where contracts could be made for house burglaries, horse and cattle thefts and even an assassination, if the price was right.

Greatly upset by the botched robbery, the killer told Tom about the failed attempt and subsequent murder of Mrs. Haynes. After relaying his grief to Tom, the killer took his gun and went to Madame Lester's saloon and brothel in the 100 block of Skiddy Street (now Chestnut Street).

The saloon building was fifty feet wide with one-story in the front and a large two-story masonry building in the rear that housed the brothel and "soiled doves." Madame Lester's brothel was one of the most popular institutions in the city and commonly attracted large crowds of rowdy men and women.

Skiddy Street as it appeared in 1891.

The killer was looking for Mrs. Haynes' half-brother, George Garner, who had allegedly helped him plan the robbery. Garner was half-Choctaw and was known to be involved in many seedy operations. He often frequented Madame Lester's brothel, where the killer hoped to locate him and seek revenge for the bungled robbery.

The killer entered the lively brothel shortly before midnight, where the pianist's music created a festive scene as the Madame tried to coax a gentleman into buying another drink. Girls and men, enjoying the evening of promiscuity, lounged around the main room. Maude Kramer, one of the working girls, was seated in a wicker chair near the center of the room and to her rear were George Garner and Alice Adams.

According to local newspapers at the time, the killer strode into the brothel with his pistol and started firing without warning. The flash and concussion of the guns startled everyone, causing a momentary silence as a hush fell over the partygoers. Rapidly, another flash was seen as the culprit began shooting at Garner from the door and hit Maude Kramer instead. Kramer, a young woman living a hard life, threw up her hands and cried out in a low, yet audible voice, "I'm shot!"

What came next was pure chaos as women screamed and men darted behind every conceivable form of cover so as not to become the next victims of the shooter. It is said that some men and women were nearly trampled trying to make their way to the exits. In the confusion, the killer was lost in the crowd and escaped.

The first bullet passed entirely through Maude Kramer, through the arm of a chair, then the dress of a woman standing near Alice Adams and George Garner before burying itself in the opposite wall near the door leading to the beer storage room. The second shot passed through Maude's stomach, finding its mark in the center of her body. The bullet's force had been spent and it fell down into the chair when Maude was removed to the upper floor of the building so a physician could be summoned to save her.

The house soon filled with a whole host of revelers who came to look upon the ghastly scene. It is at this time, that news of Mrs. Haynes' demise reached the city, causing a flurry of activity and speculation about the shooter who had his grip on the city and her citizens.

A rather odd event followed the shooting at Madame Lester's. A man with a heavy mustache, dark clothing, square shoulders, and a rather striking appearance arrived at the front door of the brothel, seeking permission to see the injured woman.

His request was denied and it was with this denial that the stranger began to act in a very peculiar manner. He withdrew a large pistol from his person and said, "The wages of sin is death," and turned to a nearby man, with gun raised, saying, and "You would make a good target".

The stranger continued to speak at some length on the wickedness of the world and appeared to be some type of ministerial crank. Upon leaving the building, he headed toward Main Street and was never seen again. He was unknown to any of the townspeople and was assumed to be a possible accomplice in the assassination.

Word spread like wildfire that a shooter was loose along Skiddy Street. Someone ran across to the Rivers Bagnio, another popular saloon and brothel, to inform the patrons of the shooting at Madame Lester's. As expected, all of the patrons and girls wanted to go have a look at the tragedy that had unfolded.

In the front, east-facing room of the Rivers bagnio was a girl by the name of Rosa Stuart and her male companion. Rosa was gathering up her outer garment by the light of a brightly burning lamp when there was a flash and a loud pop, followed by the girl sinking to the floor with a stream of blood gushing out from the right lower breast and another on the opposite side behind.

The window shade in the room had not been completely lowered, leaving a crack of about two inches near the bottom of the shade and the windowsill. It was through this crack that the bullet passed into the room.

The doctor had just completed dressing the wounds of Maude Kramer when he was summoned to the Rivers bagnio to aid the quickly perishing Rosa. Everything was done to save the young woman, but it looked as if the outcome would be a grim death.

With three shootings so far, the residents of the city began to panic. Men armed themselves and waited at their homes with their families for the next attack. The Stanley Rangers and the

Denison Rifles were mustered out and every stranger on the streets was stopped and thoroughly searched.

Two officers by the name of Preston and Deering were stationed at the office of the Star Lumber Yard, just in case the killer came that way. In not much time, a suspicious character was seen, and when the officers called for him to surrender for searching, the man turned rapidly and fled.

The officers pursued the man, firing four shots, but the man proved too fast and disappeared into the darkness near the north approach of the viaduct. His identity was never known.

While people were still gathered in the 100 block of West Skiddy Street, where the two young prostitutes had been shot, a courier from North Denison approached and announced that another shooting had taken place in the 200 block of West Morton Street. The time of the announcement is placed at 3:20 am and shows how rapidly the succession of shootings and death spread across the 20-year-old town.

The next victim was a young organist at St. Patrick's Catholic Church. Mrs. Hawley, a widow, and her daughters, Florentine "Teen" and Allie, had come to Denison from Shreveport, Louisiana and had only lived in the city about eight months; four of those months were in a brick cottage on Morton Street.

Teen Hawley was an accomplished young woman, described as modest, refined, and highly respected by the community. She and her sister were rapidly ascending the social ladder of

Denison and were often welcomed as members in the city's elite social circles.

The 200 block of West Morton ca. 1890

That fateful night, the family retired as usual, not knowing that a killer was loose in their normally sleepy neighborhood. Mrs. Hawley occupied a small bedroom on the northwest side of the home, while the girls slept in an adjoining room to the east. The doorway leading from Mrs. Hawley's room opened into the kitchen as well as into the girls' room.

Two boarders, a man by the name of Mr. Kellogg and Watt Smith, of the MK&T civil engineering corps, rented front bedrooms in the small home. Kellogg was away at work and Smith was in his room asleep at the time of the mischief.

Close to 3 am, a noise coming from the kitchen awakened Allie, who saw the form of a man approaching her bed. In the dim light, she was able to make out a pistol in one hand of the man and a knife in the other.

Allie began to scream but was quickly silenced by the man who commanded her to keep quiet or be killed. She begged him saying, "Take anything you want, if you can't find it, I will get it for you. I don't want you to wake my sister; she is very excitable and will go into hysterics."

The armed intruder replied, "I'll do worse than that. I'm going to kill her." It was at this point that Allie let out a piercing scream and was able to jump out of bed and evade the intruder. A noise in an adjoining room frightened the man who fled the scene.

Both young women were terribly frightened, and Teen jumped out of her bed. The intruder turned and fired back into the girls' room, but the bullet missed and buried itself in the brick wall on the opposite end of the room.

By this time, both girls were hysterical, and Teen ran into her mother's room to seek comfort. Mrs. Hawley put her arms around her eldest daughter and tried to console her. Smith, the male border, was awakened by the shot and searched the house for the intruder. Seeing no sign of him, Smith locked the doors and windows, assuring the women that the man was gone.

Just when all seemed back to normal, a bullet came whizzing through one of the windows, striking Teen just below the right shoulder blade, making a ghastly wound through her body. She fell forward and died instantly.

Neighboring men were awakened by the shooting and screams from the Hawley house and ran out into the night to offer assistance. A man was seen in the backyard of the home, but he ran away through a rear gate when asked to stop. It was reported that the man ran down the alley east of Morton Street and north on Austin Avenue to the alley between Morton Street and Bond Street.

Men on foot and on horseback began searching the area and beating the alleys and streets in every part of town, clinging to the hope that they would find the killer. However, their attempts were in vain, and it was determined that the murderer had either hidden well or escaped all together.

Panic and terror seized the city where no one could conceive such a horrible situation in any community or city. Four women had been shot as though they were targets for a sportsman's practice. At that time, two were dead and the other two were barely clinging to life. Maude Kramer, Madame Lester's girl, soon died of her injuries, leaving Rosa Stuart as the only survivor of that fateful night.

By Wednesday morning, every motorcar brought friends and sympathizers to the Haynes' home, and a burial service was planned. Florentine "Teen" Hawley was dressed in a black burial robe and laid in the parlor of her mother's house for members of the community to say their final goodbyes before her burial on Thursday. Throughout all of this, the question of the mysterious shooter was brought up in nearly every locale in the city.

The murder of Mrs. Haynes' indicated that a fumbled robbery had occurred, yet no evidence of robbery was found at the other crime scenes. Officers did believe that the shootings were the work of one man, as all bullets fired came from the same .44-caliber revolver.

It was rumored that a local gambler by the name of Dick Edwards had dated Teen Hawley at one time, and tried to dispose of the Mrs. Haynes' jewelry in Dallas. Supposedly, he was to take the rings and earrings to a Madame in Dallas, where they would be sold or pawned by the Madame. It appeared that the Madame double-crossed Edwards, and instead of getting rid of the jewelry, went to the local Dallas police.

It would be February of 1893 before Edwards would finally be caught in Duluth, Minnesota. He was arrested and brought back to Sherman to stand trial for the murder of Mrs. Haynes. All evidence was circumstantial, so the death penalty could not be pursued. However, he was found guilty and sentenced to life in prison.

Edwards died of pneumonia in a Sherman jail soon after his sentencing, and never carried out even part of his sentence. His attorney was later able to prove that Edwards was out of town on the night the murders occurred.

Mrs. Haynes was buried in her father's cemetery plot in

Fairview Cemetery while Florentine "Teen" Hawley was buried in Calvary Cemetery, owned by St. Patrick's Catholic Church. The Hawley's left Denison shortly after the funeral and burial ceremony and were never heard from again.

The gravesite of Mrs. Hattie Haynes, the first victim of the Night of Terror.

Madame Lester paid to have Maude Kramer buried in Oakwood Cemetery, but an old sweetheart from Ironton, Missouri heard of her murder and paid to have her remains disinterred and shipped back home for a burial under her real name, Alta McIntosh.

Ike Lindsay, a local mortician, handled the disinterment. He awaited nightfall and dug up the grave by the light of a lantern. During the course of his work, Lindsay fell into the grave and broke several ribs.

The three murders remain unsolved to this day, although there have been many theories as to the true murderer of the night of terror. These murders would result in hauntings that still occur in present day.

In February of 1912, a local banker named Russel S. Legate moved the Haynes house from the 2500 block of Woodlawn Boulevard to 310 West Gandy Street, near the Denison Public Library. During the move, the massive home hit the cables of the Southwestern Telegraph and Telephone Company, knocking out service for many subscribers in the southwest part of town. One of the cables fell onto the Traction Company's trolley wire and was burned in two with a glare that lit up the whole street.

The two-story home had to rest in the middle of the intersection of Mirick Avenue and Main Street until the wires could be moved. While there, many local residents and children went to see the large home placed precariously in the middle of the busy thoroughfare. Loud noises could be heard coming from the home and many claimed to see the figure of a woman moving throughout the abandoned residence, earning the home the title of haunted house.

The library eventually expanded, and the home was lost to the ravages of time. However, people still report seeing a woman, dressed in her finest Victorian apparel, complete with earrings and other fine jewelry, wandering amongst the stacks. Is it possible that Hattie Haynes was never able to leave her home?

Could she still be with us, walking amongst the books in search of answers for her untimely demise?

Another of those women among us who witnessed such a tragic end is Maude Kramer, the soiled dove of Madame Lester's brothel. It is believed that her ghost still haunts the area in which she was killed. In the basement of 119 West Main, a figure appears in all the finery of the late 1800's. This building, housing the present-day Vitina's Deli, was still in existence when Maude met her demise and was discussed in a previous chapter.

It is said that she haunts the locale because of its familiarity to her mortal life. While never a bothersome presence, she can catch you off guard. The faint figure of a woman has also been seen in the alleyways of the 100 block of Main and Chestnut Streets, as if she continues the search for her eternal home.

Chapter Eleven

UFO Sightings
Lights in the Skies

UFO's, formally known as "Unidentified Flying Objects", "Flying Saucers," and all other various names for objects in the sky, have been around for many years and still draw the attention and curiosity of people all over the world.

An article in the *Denison Daily News* from January 25, 1878 tells of one such "sighting" of a strange phenomenon by a local farmer, John Martin. He claimed he was out hunting one evening when he noticed a dark object high in the northern sky. The odd-shaped object seemed to speed up and the farmer had to strain his eyes to try to get a closer look.

The farmer stated that he watched the object for so long that he became momentarily blinded and had to look away for a few minutes to rest his eyes. When he finally looked back, the object, which had appeared so distant, was now nearly directly overhead, and he described it as a large saucer. The object quickly disappeared into the southern sky and no more was ever seen of it. This is known as the first time the term "flying saucer" was used in a report.

On July 15, 1953, a reported UFO sighting occurred at Perrin Air Force Base, now known as the North Texas Regional Airport at Perrin Field. Crewmen on the base witnessed several unknown objects flying in the sky.

Perrin Air Force Base Entrance ca 1946.

The formation of the seven unknown objects was described to appear in the shape of a "Z" with three on the top, one in the middle, and three on the bottom. The lights quickly peeled away from their formation one by one and spiraled up into space.

A one-page report of the sighting was sent from Perrin to the Pentagon, the Air Defense Command, the CIA and other institutions on July 25, 1953. The report was classified at the time but was declassified in the early 2000's.

Perrin Air Force Base during the early 1940's.

The report includes various information that ground control observed seven unidentified objects with one bright red light on each object. It states that the objects, visually observed by both the Perrin tower along with citizens of Denison and Sherman, hovered at estimated altitudes of five to eight thousand feet. No air-to-air contact was made and no radar contact was made with Perrin radar. Visual contact was made from 9:39 pm to 9:55 pm with unlimited visibility and clear sky conditions.

Some have discounted the report as some flyboys attempting to have some fun. However, local newspapers at the time reported that many others in the area had witnessed the light as well, leading most to believe that the accounts were factual and that something truly did light up the sky that night.

Another sighting took place around 1956 when a local man and his wife were returning home from an evening in the Mockingbird Lane area of Northwest Denison. As they were getting out of their vehicle, they saw several flying objects, at the top of the hill, circling each other and trading places from top to bottom.

The commotion drew the attention of eight neighbors and the couple's parents, who all claimed to have witnessed the display as well which continued for several minutes before the objects split up and flew away.

Another instance occurred around that same time when a young woman and her husband went to visit her parents living on Snow Road, southeast of Denison. The woman claimed that she, her husband, her parents, as well as her brother and his wife were relaxing on the screened-in porch on the east side of the house and enjoying the night sky. Suddenly, red lights appeared in the south and began moving toward the north at a rapid rate of speed.

The group said the lights seemed to be evenly spaced and quite high in the sky, but not as high as an airplane would normally fly. The lights crossed over the house and began to ascend higher into the air, one by one. In all, there were thought to be nine lights with four in front and five behind, spaced like bowling ball pins.

In May of 1971, seven people reported spotting strange UFO-like objects around the Texomaland area. One Denison man got such a good look at the object that he was able to draw a sketch. He drew a saucer like structure with lighted portholes and fire streaming in sparks from the rear with green and yellow pulsating lights.

All of these instances and sightings took place over several decades, leading one to believe that this is no isolated incident. Is it possible that there are strange objects flying around Denison? If so, where will they crop up next; who will be the next witnesses to this unique part of our city's history?

Chapter Twelve

Cutter's Dance Hall
Denison's Haunted Night Club

Once one of the Texoma Area's premier entertainment venues, Cutter's Dance Hall also played a part as one of our area's most haunted sites. The popular dance hall and nightclub was located at 4331 South Texoma Parkway and has since been sold and remodeled into a glass-manufacturing site.

Employees reported having bad feelings in parts of the building that caused their hair to stand on end. Others reported lights turning on and off, and one creepy instance of a ladder being folded out in the middle of a room where the ladder had not previously been located. Ethereal sounds and equipment malfunctions were a huge part of the haunting that occurred at this site.

So much attention was drawn to the area, that a local news channel, KTEN, took a crew from the Ghost Hunters of Southern Texoma (G.H.O.S.T.) to investigate. While there, they heard strange knocking at doors when no one was around. They also experienced doors opening and closing on their own as well as reports of strange moving shapes and objects throughout different parts of the building.

It has been said that the hauntings have quieted down some now that the establishment has changed and no longer has dancing or alcohol available. Was it a patron, waiting for the last call? Or could the spirit still be lingering, simply dormant and waiting for the party to start again?

Cutters as it appeard before undergoing an extensive interior and exterior remodel.

Chapter Thirteen

The Miller House
The Return of the Native

At the corner of Walker Street and Brown Avenue, there sits an old home that does not quite match those surrounding it. The home predates many around it by dozens and dozens of years and was one of the first homes built near what would become Denison.

James Kinsey Miller, commonly referred to as J.K., arrived in Texas in 1852 following a two-month trip by wagon train from Macon County, North Carolina. Traveling with Miller were his wife, Orenna Taboe Miller, whom he had married six years prior, and their children. The couple would have 12 children throughout the early years of their marriage.

The Miller's originally settled five miles west of Sherman but moved to the area that Denison would soon occupy in 1860. The enterprising family built a log cabin on the banks of a spring that would become known locally as Miller's Springs. The location for the new home was also advantageous because it was near Baer's Ferry that crossed the Red River. Two more children would be born while the family lived in the home, bringing the total to 14 children.

The log home was built atop a stone cellar that had been constructed as a fortress with holes along the walls where rifles could be placed in the event of an Indian raid. It is said that Miller traded 50 to 125 ponies to the Caruthers family for his 165-acre spread.

Before Denison could be developed, Miller wanted his family to have religion as a part of their daily lives, so he built a church and baptistery for personal use. He named the church Mount Pleasant Baptist that would grow to become the present-day Mount Pleasant Baptist Church that is still very active in the Denison community.

Miller built a log schoolhouse for his children and is also said to have grown cotton where the present-day Main Street Mall is at 500 West Main Street.

Once, Miller's wife was going down to the spring for water and came upon an Indian with a broken leg. She tore her apron into strips, made a splint for his leg, and even nursed him for a time until he was strong enough to return to his village.

The Miller House at the corner of Walker Street and Brown Avenue.

After that, the Millers would find either a deer, turkey, or other kill on their back porch around the Thanksgiving and Christmas holidays.

This tradition continued for decades, long after the Indians had relocated to parts of Oklahoma, and even after the original Miller family had passed away. Was this benevolent gesture, which continued for much longer than the Indian could have lived, a gift from the afterlife?

Of interesting note, Miller's Spring dried up when the nearby Safeway Corporation constructed a warehouse on a portion of land close to the Miller homestead. Once the spring stopped flowing, so did the gifts of wild game that had always been left on the porch. Perhaps the benevolent spirit left when the springs dried up, or maybe it is still around the neighborhood waiting for the springs to start back up again.

The Safeway plant that was constructed over Miller's Spring, causing it to stop flowing.

The house still stands today at 1401 West Walker, although it was encased in stone at some point so it no longer has the look and style of a log cabin. The foyer is where the dogtrot used to run through the home and additional rooms and a porch have been added over the years. The fortified cellar is still in existence, although the floor was dug out an additional eighteen inches, concrete added, and drywall put up to make the area into a game room.

Chapter
Fourteen

The Hotel Denison
The Guests that Never Left

The Hotel Denison that we know today was not the first for our city. The first true hotel in Denison was located at 500 West Main and was originally built as the Denison Commercial College, sometimes referred to as the National Commercial College.

The school opened for its first session on September 1, 1891 and was hailed as the largest commercial college in the country.

The impressive building was styled with Victorian gingerbread elements, arched windows, and an elegant cupola. The sides fronting Main Street and Fannin Avenue were constructed of St. Louis pressed brick with the first floor containing three large vestibules finished with elegant tilework.

With over 36,000 square feet of floor space, the Commercial College was billed as one of the largest such institutions in the country. Classes at the new educational facility included bookkeeping, business arithmetic, commercial law, banking, insurance, real estate, and a variety of other courses.

Some of Denison's most respected citizens served on the board for the fledgling school, and the entire community had great hope that the college would flourish. However, that was never meant to be.

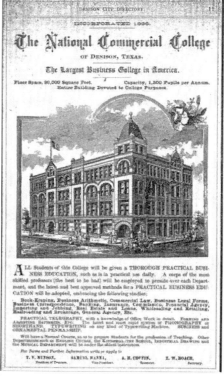

An advertisement for the new Commercial College ca 1890.

Through various failures on behalf of the Commercial College, coupled with the Panic of 1893, the school was closed and all classes ceased. The building would not remain empty for long, though, as it was soon retrofitted to become Denison's largest hotel, known as the Hotel Denison. The hostelry prospered for many years before it met its demise on a cold wintry night.

The newly christened Hotel Denison ca 1895.

The grand and imposing four-story brick structure went up in a blaze of glory on the night of January 24, 1920. Firefighters were handicapped in putting out the fire after one of the pumping engines broke down during the blaze. This pump failure ultimately led to the demise of the entire structure, along with several businesses that adjoined the hotel.

An article in the *San Antonio Even News* from January 26, 1920 stated that the debris of the Denison Hotel had been searched and no bodies could be found amongst the wreckage.

It was deemed a miracle that everyone in the hotel, filled to capacity with nearly 700 guests, was able to escape safely. However, mysterious appearances (note a previous story at the current Main Street Mall location) at the site of the old hotel lead people to believe that not all made it out safely.

Searching through debris is often very difficult to do, and without a guest list of those in the hotel, it is possible that someone was overlooked and perished in the flames. One of the neighboring businesses that was also destroyed was a funeral home and casket warehouse. Although no mention was ever made, it is possible that there were bodies awaiting burial in the funeral home that were never properly laid to rest.

The Hotel Denison on the morning of January 25, 1920.

The damage to the hotel and the 500 block of West Main was deemed catastrophic. The hotel was the finest and largest building in downtown Denison and left the city without any first-class hotel services following the fire.

The need for a new hotel was quickly realized and when private financing was not an option, the Denison Chamber of Commerce opted for a hometown project, financed and run by the people of Denison. The Chamber was able to contract with Arthur Simpson and Joseph Crumpton to build a gleaming new hotel that would make the city and her citizens proud.

Simpson was a native of Denison, and Crumpton immigrated to the city in 1909 from Illinois. The two men were in-laws and business partners in the nearby Palace Hotel, located at the southwest corner of Main Street and Burnett Avenue. The two men also owned numerous properties throughout the city, including the proposed location for the new hotel. Plans for the project were officially announced on September 4, 1923.

Barnett, Haynes and Barnett of St. Louis were the architects tasked with the design of the new hotel. The firm was responsible for such feats as the Palace of Liberal Arts for the Louisiana Purchase Exposition, the Cathedral Basilica of St. Louis, and the opulent Adolphus Hotel in Dallas. The hotel design for Denison was one of the final designs the firm completed before dissolving in 1930.

The architects' illustrations called for a six-story building with an estimated cost of $222,942.80, not including furnishings. The modern structure's exterior would consist of sandstone blocks with buff Bedford terracotta trim on the first floor with red brick and terra cotta trim on the facings of the upper stories. A decorated frieze of stone would provide a crowning cornice atop the building.

Sandstone window frames would hold leaded glass on the first floor with the top of the first-floor windows to contain custom pieces of stained glass. Following the ruin of the city's first hotel, the new edifice would be fireproof with walls and floors of concrete with the final addition being an elegant iron canopy projecting over the hotel's main entrance on Burnett Avenue.

Work officially began at 2:10 pm on September 6, 1923, when the Secretary of the Chamber of Commerce, J.E.T. Peters, climbed to the top of Beazley's garage, the building occupying the site that the hotel would be constructed on, pried a brick loose from the façade and tossed it to the ground below. Construction had just begun when it was decided to add a seventh floor of penthouse suites to the plan.

Craftsmen from all over North Texas and the surrounding area took part in the construction. D.B. Ridpath of Ardmore did the excavation and poured the concrete; Charles Schley of Denison assembled the brickwork and terra cotta trim; painting and interior decoration went to W.H. Crutcher of Dallas and all millwork in the new building was designed and installed by Waco Sash and Door.

DENISON HAS NEW SEVEN-STORY HOTEL

An article from The Dallas Morning News on April 22, 1924 shows the progress of the new hotel.

The extensive tilework, terrazzo, and marble enhancements came from J. Desco & Son of Dallas with J.C. Korioth of Sherman handling the heating and plumbing for the enormous building.

The newly christened Hotel Simpson opened to enormous fanfare on October 1, 1924 with an open house and ball that lasted from 12 noon until 12 midnight.

Through various changes in management over the years, the building was renamed Hotel Denison and operated under that name until it closed in the latter half of the 20th century. Now privately owned and used as apartments, the building sits in a state of decay and despair.

The once-grand hotel still maintains some of its original charm despite the lack of care and upkeep throughout the years. The wood in the lobby is all Douglas fir and much of the antique furniture in the lobby was there when the hotel opened in 1924. The grand staircase across from the elevators leads to the mezzanine floor that was available for use by women at the hotel.

The "ladies of the evening" would sit in this area with windows over the intricately carved front registration desk. The women would try to solicit business from gentlemen in the lobby below then take them across the over-the-alley sky bridge to 404 West Main Street, a local brothel, which contained a series of small rooms. Another "unofficial" service available to hotel guests was bootleg liquor that could be brought by bellhops during prohibition.

The first floor, which contains the lobby, ballroom, coffee room, dining salon, five store spaces, six sample rooms, and a porters' room still features the original Otis elevators from the opening that are still in operation. The penthouse suites featured such noted guests as Rosemary Clooney and Jose Ferrer, Gene Autry, Roy Rogers, Tex Ritter, Harry Houdini and President Eisenhower.

Houdini was quoted in the Denison Herald on October 14, 1924 as saying, "It is a great pleasure to me to pay for my room in this magnificent hotel It was beyond my expectations, and nowhere, in my travels, have I found a hotel any better equipped and with better accommodations."

The Hotel Simpson (later Denison) ca. 1930.

While the hotel was in its heyday, thousands of patrons visited for dinner, elegant balls and parties, and to stay as overnight guests. Is it possible that some guest checked in, but never checked out? Strange occurrences at Denison's tallest building have had locals talking for many years.

People have reported seeing a person standing in the window of the fifth floor, looking out onto the city below. The figure is seen often at night and appears in the windows on the Chestnut Street side of the building. This would not seem out of place in a building occupied by apartments; however, the fifth floor is vacant and has remained that way for decades.

Other occurrences include lobby furniture moved around, lights flickering on and off along the corridors, and music coming from the abandoned ballroom. Could the figure and strange occurrences be attributed to a guest with unfinished business at the hotel?

One theory on the haunting, that is certainly possible, deals with one of the hotel's most magical guests. The great Harry Houdini passed away from complications arising from a burst appendix in October of 1926, just a few short years after visiting the Hotel Denison. His gravesite has been desecrated and vandalized over the years, possibly causing unrest.

Houdini described the accommodations at the hotel as very favorable; perhaps they became his final resting place. Could he be the figure in the window? Could the occurrences around the hotel be his mischief?

Chapter Fifteen

Waples United Methodist Church
The Vigilant Parishioner

Several different religious denominations began to sprout up in Denison rather quickly after the town was founded; one of the first to bud was the Methodist Episcopal Church South.

As the town grew, more and more people began making Denison a permanent residence rather than a stop along the railroad lines, and by 1886, the city had a population of approximately 11,000. With the influx of all different people entering the town, more establishments were needed and more churches sprouted up to better serve the growing population.

One church in particular was willing to brave the undesirable red-light district, known as Skiddy Street, to help spread

Christianity throughout the fledgling city; that church would eventually come to be known as Waples United Methodist Church.

Southern Methodism had its first entrance into Denison's history in 1873 when a Mr. Ball came when a Mr. Ball arrived in Denison with the intention of completing a census to determine how many citizens were Methodists. Ball's trip to Denison was a success and he was able to find some 40 citizens who were of the Methodist denomination. On March 14, 1873, Reverend Alexander Jamison was sent by Bishop Wiley to Denison to represent the missionary Board of the Methodist Episcopal Church and organize a church in Denison.

In March of 1875, the Southern Methodists began to seek bids for the erection of a house of worship that was to be located at 430 W. Skiddy Street. Shortly thereafter, the new mission church was complete and ready for worship services. The mission church began under the leadership of Reverend Z. Parker and was a mission project of the North Texas Conference of the Methodist Episcopal Church South.

The church was a one-room style building with a bell tower. The mission on Skiddy Street continued as a mission church until 1881 when it was granted an official charter. By this time, Methodism had gained such a following within the city that it was no longer deemed a mission and became a true church of Denison with its first regular pastor, Reverend C.I. McWhister.

The first building of the Methodist Episcopal Church, South on Skiddy Street.

On January 13, 1881 in order for the mission to become a church in the Methodist Episcopal Conference, the church building was purchased by the conference at a sum of $200 to make it an official asset of the Methodist Episcopal Church rather than a mission church.

The Methodist Episcopal churches in Texas in 1887 were growing so rapidly that it led to the organization of an annual conference in many areas including the Sherman-Denison Conference.

Around 1887, Mr. and Mrs. E.B. Waples, for whom the church is named in memory of, became members of the young Methodist congregation. Mr. Waples came to Texas in 1877 and resided in Sherman for the first ten years that he lived in Texas before settling in Denison in 1887.

He became a senior partner in the grocery firm of Waples, Platter & Company, and also had a large interest in the Bluff City Lumber Company. Mr. Waples and his wife were strict members of the Methodist Episcopal Church South, and were regarded by the citizens of Denison as "two of the most upright and valuable members of the community".

On December 31, 1888, the Trustees of the Methodist Church executed a note to Mr. Waples in the amount of $1,692.76 bearing ten percent interest and secured by a mortgage on the property. On March 5, 1891, the note amounting to $1,692.76 (plus $540 in interest) was released to the church on the payment of only $1.00 to Mr. Waples.

Southern Methodism continued to grow in Denison until the congregation quickly outgrew the first church building, and in 1898 plans for the main auditorium of a new church began. Under the pastorate of Reverend P.C. Archer, the members of the church began to make plans to construct this new sanctuary so as to give the congregation a larger place of worship.

The new building was to be located at 830 West Main Street and to be constructed of red brick. The site chosen for the new church was significant because it was the site of the first permanent residence in Denison; this residence was established by Dr. Morrison and was a one-room log cabin.

Construction quickly began on a beautiful brick structure with stained glass windows that would serve as a beacon on Main

Street in the still young "Gate City" known as Denison. Sadly, Mr. Waples died on October 4, 1898, and was not able to witness the completion of the church, yet he did live long enough to see the foundation of the new structure completed.

The Waples Methodist Church building at Main and Scullin from 1899 – 1965.

As Mr. Waples lay in his deathbed, he called his children to him, and said, "I will shortly lay down the thread of life and if you children do not take up where I left off and finish this building and support of this church, Southern Methodism will get a setback in Denison that will take years to overcome."

It was at this time that he gave the first monetary gift towards the new church structure in the amount of $3,000. His children and grandchildren remained steadfast in their support of the church and construction was completed in April of 1899.

The new building was heralded as the finest church in North Texas with its tall spires and stained-glass windows. The purity and richness of the colors of the stained glass within the church were due to the art of European glasscutters. The light fixtures were made of heavy brass hoops with seven individual brass shades attached.

At this time, a bishop of the Methodist Episcopal Church South, Bishop Key, visited the congregation and told them, "This church is here today because of the faith and effort of Mr. and Mrs. Waples and I want to see it named Waples Memorial Methodist Church, South." And from then on the Methodist Episcopal Church South of Denison was no more and was replaced with Waples Memorial Methodist Church, South.

In 1910, a Sunday school was started in the church and soon thereafter an Epworth League was formed. Within the next several years, the church began to flourish at its new location, and there was no longer room in the main auditorium to house both the Sunday school and the rest of the membership.

During this time an addition was added to the main auditorium of the church in order to accommodate the quickly growing Sunday school classes. The debt for the addition was cancelled in 1920 under the leadership of the pastor, Charles W. Hearon.

A view of Waples Methodist Church, ca. 1920's.

As the church continued to grow, so did its campus of buildings. In 1924, plans for an even larger education building were started and a lot directly east of the church was purchased. The final plans for the new education edifice were finished in April of 1926. In June of 1926, a campaign was begun to help raise the necessary $50,000 for the erection of the new education building.

Construction began on the two story cream-colored brick structure with basement on August 26, 1927, and was completed in August of 1928. A long time business partner and in-law to Mr. Waples, Mr. A. F. Platter, was instrumental in the planning and financing of the new addition to the church.

During the beginning stages of the construction of the new building, Mr. Platter pledged $12,500 towards the cost of the construction, and in June of 1927 he again gave the church another $12,500 towards the education building.

A view of Waples showing the education wing at left, ca. 1960's.

When approximately $18,000 in debt remained on the education building, two church members, Mr. and Mrs. Kline, left all their money to the church to pay off the note and clear away all debt on the newly completed building. All they asked in return for their donation was for their portrait to be hung in the building so that they would never be forgotten. Their request was maintained and as of today their portrait still hangs in the church.

Waples began its proud sponsorship of Boy Scout Troop 605 in 1936. This sponsorship continues today with one of the largest Boy Scout Troops in Denison. In 1938 and 1939, the Northern and Southern Methodist Episcopal Churches of Denison merged and many of the members from the First Methodist Church joined the Waples Methodist Church as a result of the merger.

The merger caused the membership of the congregation to grow exponentially, and by the end of 1938 the congregation had a membership of 890. Through the years that followed the church continued to grow and serve the community, the church choir donned beautiful robes, and a weekly newsletter and church bulletin were printed and handed out at each Sunday service.

In 1955, a remodeling program was begun at the church and for the first time since the church was constructed, air conditioning became a part of the services. Other improvements were made and it was the hope of the congregation that this massive remodeling program would be sufficient to maintain the church's structural integrity. But as the church congregation continued to grow, the use of the building became more and more limited. Soon, cracks began to show on the structure and the roof began to leak.

In 1962, the R.L. Roth engineering firm was called to the church to do an inspection of the sanctuary and educational building. They wrote in response to their inspection: "We have inspected the sanctuary unit and the education unit of your church facilities and in our opinion the sanctuary has reached a state beyond which further investment in repairs and maintenance is economically unsound. Therefore, the most practical long-range solution would be to demolish the building and rebuild a modern structure for present and future needs."

The present church edifice was built in 1965 under the pastorate of Reverend Walter L. Underwood. There was an immense building campaign to help raise money for the new church and record amounts of pledges were received. It was noted that the one-million-dollar debt on this new building was reduced to just $100,000 within seven years of the erection of the new building.

Sadly, the old church edifice was removed from the lot and the present building sits on the site of the red brick building. The present edifice is over-flowing with a bevy of Christian symbols that were incorporated into the construction of the building.

Waples UMC as it appears today.

The marble walls and slate floors of the Narthex reflect ever-lasting life and the eternal character of God. Inside the sanctuary, the marble alter table is etched with symbols of the sacraments of the Lord's Supper including grapes, wheat, and chalice.

The church boasts one-of-a-kind liturgical banners which reflect different seasons of the Christian religion. The banners were designed by Jane Lundergan Doak and were hand sewn by women of the church. The lectern contains the emblems of the four gospels of the New Testament: Matthew, Mark, Luke, and John. The pulpit contains the Greek symbols Chi and Rho which are the first two letters of the word Christ. The communion rail is supported by twelve carvings that contain the insignias of the twelve disciples, all except for Judas.

The stained glass that can be found throughout the sanctuary and Madden Chapel was created, designed, and fabricated by the internationally famous artist Gabriel Loire of Chartres, France. The large stained-glass window in the sanctuary contains the cross with descending dove, the Star of David, the crown of thorns, and the symbols for the Alpha and Omega.

The copper bell tower and spire rise from the center of the sanctuary to a height of 90 feet above the ground. Within the bell tower is the original bell from the first mission church on Skiddy Street.

The Boy Scout Troop 605 Scout Hut was built adjacent to Waples in 1970 shortly after the new church was completed. This was a huge leap for the scout troop that had previously met in the church basement of the 1899 structure, and then met inside of a house adjacent to the newly constructed 1965 structure.

The hut was built on a lot adjacent to the church, and was erected in memory of Mr. Charles H. Harris and family, following the receipt of a gift to the church. The current scout hut was expanded in 2003 thanks in part to a generous grant from the Clara Blackford Smith and W. Aubrey Smith Charitable Foundation.

Waples has sponsored its own day school since its inception in 1964. The first classes were held in a small house where the present-day Scout Hut is located, and the first teachers of the newly formed day school were Mrs. Pauline Sullenberger, mother of the famous pilot Chesley Sullenberger, and Mrs. Karen Hibbit.

The purpose of the school was to provide classes for kindergarten and pre-school aged children of all races and backgrounds. This purpose continues today with an energized teaching staff that is willing to carry on the mission of expanding young minds.

With the quickly growing and expanding Day School, and an influx of new members into the congregation, it became necessary to once again add on to the church. On February 19, 1989, the congregation of Waples announced that it would begin its $560,000 expansion project towards the construction of a 6,000 square foot education facility, memorial garden and remodeling of the south entrance to the church.

The extension of a larger education wing and the addition of the Underwood Memorial Garden were completed in 1990. The new education wing houses the Charles K. Pool Youth Suite and is the campus for the recently formed Rotational Sunday School for all young grade-level children.

All of these changes, additions, and new building campaigns have made Waples into one of the largest structures on Main Street and one of the best examples of architecture from the 1960's. However, Waples, although new compared to most downtown structures, does still have its share of ghostly doings.

The church staff, along with several members of the congregation, have witnessed the figure of a man walking throughout the hallways of the building. He is always described as wearing a grey suit with a matching grey hat, but his face is never distinguishable. He is seen walking through the sanctuary and has walked by the window of the church office many times, but each time staff go to investigate, the figure is gone.

One church member was sitting in the sanctuary when they heard the voice of a man say, "Excuse me." Upon turning, they realized they were the only person in the entire room and a thorough search revealed no one in that portion of the building.

The author has always attended services at this location, and during the days of youth group meetings on Sunday nights, he would help the Youth Director, along with other youth, to lock up the church building after turning off all of the lights.

One of the lights was on in the day school bathroom on the east side of the building. The youth group turned off the light and continued to make their way around the building. When they got to the west side to turn off the final lights, a glance across the courtyard revealed that the light in the bathroom from earlier was back on. None of the youth was brave enough to go back so the light was deemed "a security light "for the evening and left on.

Some speculate that the figure is that of Captain Waples, who did not live to see the church complete and named for him. Others think it is the spirit of someone whose home used to occupy part of the land the church was expanded on. No matter who it is, the stories do make for an interesting time during church lock-ins with the youth group.

Chapter

Sixteen

The Denison Herald
The Workers that Remained

Denison has never been without a newspaper since the city was formed in 1872. The very first in the area was *the Red River Journal,* printed in red ink, for the residents of Red River City, just north of what would become Denison.

A weekly paper was established in 1872 and was originally published in a small room of unseasoned boards in the 300 block of Skiddy Street (now Chestnut Street). *The Denison News* followed soon after in 1876 in a two-story brick building located at 112 West Main. June 1882 saw the addition of *The*

Denison Morning Herald-News followed quickly by the *Denison Evening Journal.*

M.M. Scholl, who would later become a justice of the pace and known locally as a "Snake Editor" started the Denison Dispatch at 212 W. Main in 1883. He was notorious for his fearless writings and sometimes-scathing articles.

Two of the most popular and prolific papers of the city's early history were the Sunday Gazetteer and Denison Daily News, managed by B.C. Murray. Established in 1872, the Daily News prospered, and the publication's circulation was sold in 1881. Murray went into the printing of posters following the sale and had the largest poster printing plant in the South. In 1883, he began publication of the Sunday Gazetteer until he retired in 1913.

The original charter for the Herald Publishing Company was issued on July 3, 1889. Publication under the name of The Denison Herald began on July 22, 1889, in a location billed as the largest and best equipped in the Southwest. Originally, the fledgling newspaper was operated by "New York interests" in the 100 block of West Main.

The Gazetteer printed a story saying, "The new Denison Herald made its appearance Monday evening containing the afternoon Associated Press dispatches, a well filled editorial page and a full and attractive local report. It is a seven column folio of attractive makeup and handsome print, and it all its features, reflects the result of brains, capital and mechanical skill."

The Denison Herald began on Main Street but for many years the paper was published in buildings located at 303 and 305 West Woodard Street. The young enterprise was struggling until Elwin A. Thompson took over the paper in 1891 and continued as publisher until his death in 1910. Thompson's widow gained control of the Herald until 1913 when a company organized by J. Lee Greer and H.E. Ellis could take over.

On August 5, 1926, a disastrous fire swept through the buildings, destroying the plant and many of the old records. The damage was totaled at $50,000 and centered mostly on the second floor, where the composing room and editorial room were located.

Not all was lost, however, because new equipment had already been ordered for a new plant that was 80 days away from completion on the corner of that block at 331 West Woodard Street.

A rush order for the new machinery was honored so publication could continue in the fire-charred quarters without any delay in service to patrons of the paper. Sadly, many of the records of the early-day newspaper were lost in the fire.

The Herald moved into its new headquarters on November 27, 1926 at the corner of Burnett Avenue and Woodard Street. The new modern edifice was fireproof and cost an estimated $125,000 to construct.

The new Denison Herald offices and headquarters shortly after completion.

The following excerpt appeared in the newspaper at the time the building was completed:

Herald Building Complete

The new home of the Herald fronts forty-three feet on Woodard Street and 11 feet on Burnett Avenue is two stories in height and is designed to carry two additional stories. The first floor consists of the business office, stock room, circulation department and pressrooms. The second floor contains the large editorial rooms, library, composing room, telegraph room and rest rooms.

The building is fireproof and is constructed of reinforced concrete with brick and hollow tile walls trimmed with stone. The concrete roof slab is covered with two inches of cork insulation to protect the interior from heat of summer and cold of winter.

The architectural style is modified Spanish Renaissance. The interior surface of the walls are plastered, the business and editorial rooms being treated in a rough textured effect reminiscent of Old Spain and in keeping with the exterior design in which the Spanish notes is emphasized by the please blend of bluffs in the rough texture of the brick. Except in the press rooms the floors are of mosaic tile, oak and maple, the pressroom floor being concrete. The windows are set in steel frames of the casement type.

The impressive structure was designed by noted architect, John Tulloch, who also designed the Rialto Theater and the Madden home on Morton Street and was constructed by Lacy & Company contractors. At that time, the Herald employed seventy-five people and was hailed as one of Denison's most outstanding business institutions.

Operation of the venerable newspaper would stay under Greer and Ellis for 30 years before being sold to the Harte-Hanks newspaper group on April 1, 1940. A massive remodeling effort took place in the 1960's and included a large addition to the east of the main building.

A cream-colored brick "skin" was added over the exterior of the historic structure in an effort to "modernize" it, causing a great loss of the buildings original detail.

The fourth ownership took place on March 1, 1988, when the Denison Herald was sold to Donrey Media, Inc., the company that also owned the nearby Sherman Democrat.

The Denison Herald name ended in August of 1996 when the two newspapers merged to form the present-day Herald Democrat.

The Herald Democrat building ca. 2013

Over time, the Herald Democrat would consolidate all offices to the Sherman location, thus abandoning the Denison building to sit in a state of ruin. After years of sitting vacant, the building was purchased by Ironroot Republic Distillery and is undergoing renovations to become a tasting room with storage for the aging of the company's distilled spirits.

The Herald Democrat building ca. 2017

There are two such ghost stories associated with the building, and they are as follows:

The Lady in Red

For many years, there was an employee at the Herald who

was an early riser and was said to have already had one to two pots of coffee by the time most of the other employees arrived to work. She was nearly always dressed in her favorite color, red, and was the top advertising salesperson for the newspaper. Always dressing in red quickly earned he the moniker "The Lady in Red." The love affair with the color red went so far that upon passing away, she was buried in a red dress.

The story goes that after she passed away, and for many years since, the Lady in Red has appeared in and around the old Herald Democrat building. A ghostly specter, always described as dressed in red, has been seen by both employees and passersby. The spirit never says anything but simply passes from one location to the next. Her most common appearances are in the evening or just after dusk, as if she's getting ready for the next days work.

The Watchful Writer

Another haunting includes a long-time Herald employee and writer. It is said that the writer would often observe people in the dark room to see what kind of photographs they were developing.

Because the room was so dark, the writer would often make his presence known to those developing film by knocking on the table or wall behind the employee. While somewhat startling to newcomers, most seasoned employees were aware that it was simply the watchful writer and weren't frightened.

Time marched on; the writer passed away, and film no longer had to be developed in the dark room. The dark room was eventually phased out and all photographs were developed digitally with the use of computers. However, that does not mean it was the end of the writer viewing the photos.

Several employees who had to go to the Herald office late at night to develop photos from football games, parades, etc. claim they still hear the writer knocking on tables. It was not uncommon for an employee to upload their photos and suddenly hear a knock on the table beside them or behind them, as if the writer wanted them to know he was watching. The employees always describe the feeling of being watched as well, further adding to the belief that it is their former peer.

With the closing of the Herald offices, it is not known if the watchful writer still roams the halls or if he has moved on. Only time will tell if the ultimate writer will keep his vigil over those working in the building.

Chapter

Seventeen

Houston Elementary School
A Most Unique Spirit

Denison has always been well known for its educational institutions. From the earliest days of the city, education has been a priority. One of the outstanding schools that Denison has is known as Houston Elementary and is located at 1100 West Morgan Street.

Originally known as the Third Ward School, the first structure was built in 1886 on the site of the present school building. In May of 1892, the Third Ward was changed to Houston School, named for long-time Texas hero, Sam Houston.

The first Third Ward School (Houston Elementary School) building in Denison.

Although Houston died in1863 and did not see the school for which he was named, he had visited the area decades earlier as a guest of Holland and Sophia Porter. In 1904, the principal was Miss Mabel Dain with teachers Miss Maude Patrick, Miss Willie Mayes and Miss Maria K. Watt. At that time, F.B. Hughes was superintendent and Houston had a total of 270 students.

The original structure served the community until 1938 when it was determined that the building was no longer viable. Initially, the city and school board voted to close Houston School and send students to a different location. Protests took place all over the area surrounding the school, and residents were successful in keeping their neighborhood school alive.

Houston Elementary in the 1930's.

Plans for a new structure were designed by Fort Worth architect, Preston M. Gerin, who also designed Terrell School at that time. The plans called for an impressive one-story structure that would eventually occupy nearly the entire block at Morgan Street and Perry Avenue.

The historic structure was torn down and replaced by the present building. While waiting for construction to come to completion, the current students were sent to Central Ward School, Peabody School, and the Waples Methodist Sunday School building so as not to disrupt their educations.

The new school would not have been possible without the fundraising efforts of Roy Finley and the merchants of Sugar Bottom, Denison's first suburban shopping site located near the school. The total cost of the building came out to $60,000 and was considered one of the model elementary schools in the State of Texas. Mr. Finley passed away before the school could be completed and the Parent Teacher Association had a large portrait of him hung on the walls of the auditorium.

Houston Elementary School, shortly after completion in 1939.

On October 16, 1939, the local newspaper reported the following:

Sam Houston School Gives Denison Best Plant in Entire North Texas

Fully completed, Sam Houston Elementary school was in operation today, giving Denison the most up-to-date ward school plant in this section of the nation.

Furniture for the new building arrived during the weekend and was placed in use today for the first time. Every piece is movable.

Floors throughout the classrooms are of oak, cut in small squares, laid over thick concrete and padding, making it easier on feet of growing children. Halls are of red concrete.

Light color shades of paint are used in all room of the building in which the sun does not shine directly and each room of the lower grades have large cloakrooms. Individual lockers are used by the older students.

One of the most modern improvements is location of the toilets and lavatory on the edge of the building with entrances outside, preventing nauseating odors from entering the classrooms.

More than 400 chairs for the auditorium were being unpacked for use, which ware of the folding type so that the floor space can be used for any type of gathering. Twenty-four folding tables will be available for banquets. Indirect colored lighting effects are available during stage presentations, doing away with glares found on old types of stages.

Houston Elementary School entrance ca. 2015

On May 12, 1948, a new addition was added to the west of the building and was built in a similar appearance to that of the existing architecture. The new addition housed seven classrooms and a cafeteria. In addition, the schoolchildren also gained a half-block more area for a playground. Longtime principal, Gregory Roman, is credited with naming the school mascot, the Bulldog, and giving the school its colors of blue and gold.

Located nearby was Walton School, a tiny schoolhouse at the corner of West Day and South Perry that served the African American students in the area. Opened in 1917, the school was named for Dave Walton, the first principal of Langston School in southeast Denison. Walton School consolidated with Houston in 1965.

Houston Elementary School auditorium ca. 2015

Over the years, the school has been updated and a library and gymnasium were added. The interior has been refurbished and windows replaced, yet the building still retains its original charm and historic character. Houston is the oldest remaining school left in use in Denison; perhaps that is why tales of hauntings are not all that unusual.

For generations, children have reported seeing the ghost of Sam Houston walking the halls of the school. He never says anything to them, but is so memorable that students still tell of their sightings long into adulthood.

The figure is described as that of an older, balding man who sometimes appears with or without a hat on. While never sinister of threatening, the figure simply walks from one end of the school to the other. Although when anything out of the ordinary occurs, such as toilets backing up or lights flickering on and off, the events are credited to Houston's ghost.

Chapter

Eighteen

Carpenter's Bluff Bridge
The Fated Lovers

The unincoporated community of Carpenter's Bluff traces its beginning as a ferry crossing named after an early-day ferry operator and settler, Earl Elijah Carpenter. Orignally from New York, Carpenter rode his horse all the way to Texas in the 1850's, seeking to make his fortune there. While the community was named for the enterprising young settler, he did not remain long and eventually ended his days in nearby Farmersville.

For a time, the area became so rough with wild saloons that it became known as "Thief Neck" since it was considered a thief neck bend in the river. The ruffians and saloons were eventually driven out by a group of concerned citizens, and the area regained its reputable name of Carpenter's Bluff.

After serving for many years as a popular ferry crossing, plans for a true bridge began in the early 1900's. The Missouri, Oklahoma and Gulf Railway Company of Texas (MO&G) began preparations for the bridge, with the hopes that it would increase freight traffic to Texas. This railroad company would eventually become known as the KOG, the Kansas, Oklahoma and Gulf Railroad.

The KO&G Railroad Station on East Main Street ca. 1920.

The large bridge spanning 1200 feet across the Red River was begun in 1910, when the grading and laying of tracks on both sides of the river had been completed, and foundation piers using rock from nearby quarries placed to make way for the bridge. Five steel trusses, a crosstie floor, and six massive concrete foundation supports were built. Plans also called for an eight-foot wide suspended structure, commonly referred to as the shelf, to be built to the east of the bridge to be used as a walkway and area for horse-drawn vehicles to cross the river.

The bridge was completed that summer at a cost of $80,000, and one of the first trains to cross carried a group of Denison busenessmen on their way to Muskogee to promote the city as "The Gateway to Texas." The side bridge was opened a few months later and it was often said that teams of horses would become so startled by passing tains that they would take off at a fast run all the way across the span.

Eventually, the age of the automobile won out over horsedrawn traffic and cars began to cross the side bridge. A fee of 25 cents was charged for wagons pulled by no more than four animals, 5 cents for horses and cattle, 15 cents for a horse and rider, a nickel for a foot passenger, two dollars for threshing machines, and 50 cents for an automobile.

By 1965, rail traffic had decreased to such a point that it was no longer feasible for the KO&G to continue to run trains across the bridge, causing them to abandon their operations. At this point ownership of the brige was acquired by the Texas & Pacific Railroad who then deeded it to Grayson and Bryan Counties to maintain. Not long after, the railroad bridge was determined to be structurally sound and was opened as an automobile bridge on the track side.

A unique feature of the bridge is that all of the cross-ties were maintained, planks were simply laid across them diagonally and a banister was installed between the traffic side and the edge of the bridge.

By 1980, planks had begun to break and splinter, posing a serious hazard to travelers. An agreement was reached between Bryan and Grayson Counties to split the cost of removing the wooden road and replacing it with concrete.

The bridge at Carpenter's Bluff, showing a figure at one end of the bridge. No one was on the bridge when this photo was taken, ca. 2010

At this time, it was discovered that one of the giant piers had developed a large cavity underneath it from rushing waters over the years. The estimated $30,000 repair was completed, again with aid from both counties. However, the shelf side of the bridge was closed to vehicular traffic creating a one-lane bridge that spanned one of the widest rivers in the region.

With the completion of a new two-lane bridge to the west in 2017, Carpenter's Bluff bridge was officialy decommissioned as a vehicular bridge and has been converted into a span that is now only accesible by pedestrians. The hope is that the bridge will someday be used to connect hiking and biking trails between Texas and Oklahoma.

Local lore claims that the bridge was part of a tragic night for two star-crossed lovers. Long known as the back door into Oklahoma and Texas, the bridge was often used by thieves, murderers, and other fugitives as a means of a quick escape. Another popular use for the bridge was for young couples, hoping to elope, to dash into Oklahoma.

In this case, the ill-fated pair was trying to sneak across the bridge so they could be married in Oklahoma. At the time, Texas required a three-day waiting period and blood work to be done before a couple could marry. Those wishing to elope traveled to Oklahoma where there were no such requirements.

The story goes that the young couple was attempting to cross the bridge late at night and had traveled nearly halfway across the bridge when suddenly a train appeared. They quickly panicked and lept from the bridge into the rushing water fifty feet below. Sadly, neither would survive.

Locals still see two figures on the bridge at times that appear to jump into the water below. Many go to take photos of the long span of bridge and it is said that if you take a photo looking towards Oklahoma from the Texas side, you can make out the figures at the halfway point of the bridge. Have the star-crossed lovers never left the site? Are they still among the old steel and wooden pieces of the bridge?

Chapter

Nineteen

The Traveler's Hotel
Denison's Oldest Hotel

The ornate and imposing structure on the East side of the railroad tracks was constructed by Captain Ernst Martin Kohl, a ranking member of the German Navy. The building has long captivated citizens of Denison due to its unique architecture and grand nature.

The enterprising young officer enlisted in the German Navy in 1873 and quickly advanced to the rank of Captain, at which post he served for fourteen years as part of the German Navy and Merchant Marines. Kohl arrived in Texas in 1884 and travled to Austin to see the contruction of the state capital building. It is said that while he was located there, he played a key role in the contruction before relocating to Denison in 1885.

Kohl was linked to the raiload industry in several different ways. He served as General Agent for the Frisco Lot and Land Company, where he brought prospective settlers to inpsect railroad-owned lands in Oklahoma. He also had an extensive collection of railroad memorabilia including original bills of lading of the first freight shipped to Denison, as well as the original Denison sign marking the first train station in the city.

Kohl was successful and well known throughout Denison, prompting him to step into the business arena of the bustling city. To do this, he would need a building that had easy access to the passing trains.

The main floor of the building was completed in 1893 and used as a saloon and mercantile store. The walls in the main rooms of the lower floor and carriage house are over two feet thick, and the limestone used in the construction was quarried from the site. Eventually, the family added three more floors to the building to create what we know today as the Traveler's Hotel.

This monumental addition , originally serving as the Kohl family's living quarters with rooms available for boarders, was started in 1908 and completed in 1911. Over 70,000 bricks were used to complete the second and third floors and one of the bricks is inscribed with the phrase, "Nov 7, 1911, seven bricks left!" Several of the bricks are also signed by the Kohl family members and workers upon completion of the building.

The 1908 addition to the Kohl home, seen during construction.

The interior of the elegant home was built to reflect the superb crafstmanship of the era. Intricate, beaded paneling encased the doors, windows, and cabinets in the second floor dining room. Legend claims it took a carpenter seven years to complete all of the woodwork in just that one room. A built-in serving buffet blends with the high mahogony wainscoting and plate rail, imparting elegance to the dining room.

Other details in the upper floors included metal ceilings with carved beams or wood strips forming grid patterns, and many doors inlcude leaded stained glass and floral etched glass. All hardware on the upper floors including doorknobs, locksets, drawer pulls, hinges, and transom controls are brass-plated copper.

The "Hotel Traveler's Home" was opened in 1929 and catered to railorad passengers and crewmen. The Traveler's Hotel was advertised as fire-proof, being of unusually sound construction with sand packed between each floor to deter the spread of flames. Sheet metal was also applied to all ceilings and steel lathe was used behind plaster walls rather than the more common wood lathe.

Located within a two-block radius of five railroad stations, the hotel gleaned a great deal of business from passengers, crewmen, and weary travelers. Rooms on the third floor were named for Kohl's children: Elis, Bertha, Erna, Ernest, and Felix, but rooms on the fourth floor all had numbers, much like a ship.

Kohl closed his grocery store and salloon in 1933 and died in 1935. The Traveler's Hotel remained in operation for a period of time before closing in 1940. The Interstate Fine Arts Society were the next tenants of the historic structure, showcasing regional art from 1949 to 1951.

Local antique dealers, the Tuckers, purchased the building and used it for storage of their growing business. In 1975, the building was sold to the Brandt family who remodeled and restored the house into a popular restaurant known as "Down By The Station".

The Traveler's Hotel as it appears today.

After several different owners, the building now remains in private hands and still retains much of its character from days gone by.

Some say they believe Captain Kohl never really left the structure. Strange sounds at the night have been known to wake up former residents of the home. Objects have also been moved in the night, sometimes with entire rooms being rearranged during the night, unbeknownst to the sleeping residents. These stories date back several decades though nothing seems to have happened lately. Could Captain Kohl have parted from this world now that his grand home is once again used as a residence? Or is he simply biding his time, waiting amongst the stone and brick that he built his life around?

Chapter

Twenty

The Denison Public Library
The Lady of the Library

For nearly 64 years in Denison's young history, the city had the distinction of being the largest city in Texas without a library. Most surrounding cities had libraries for citizens to use, but somehow Denison had not had the support to open a library for the public.

This all changed in 1935 when the Junior Alpha Delphi Club saw the need for a public library, and began to gather books as part of their project. The main idea for the project is atributed to Clarence Johnson who had to frequently travel to Sherman for any type of reference work and research.

The largest support came from one of Denison's premier benefactors, Miss Eloise Munson. Miss Munson offered her family's historic homestead at 231 North Rusk Avenue rent-free for the first two years. The home was one of the oldest brick homes in the city and was considered one of Denison's showplaces when it was finished.

The historic Munson home at 231 North Rusk Avenue.

The Jr. Delphians quickly began working to organize interested citizens and appealed to the city government for support of the library. While originally hesitant, the city eventually agreed to spend $100 to repair the roof of the

Munson home. The local garden club also agreed to take over maintenance of the grounds around the home.

A fundraising drive was kicked off with a large meeting and carnival. Local Boy Scouts helped collect books and magazines, and Mrs. Pauline Jordan, the high school librarian, directed the cataloging. Grayson County provided two relief workers from the county library division of the WPA to aid in building up the library.

The Junior Delphians did most of the work of cleaning and repairing the Munson home and on November 22, 1935, the library was formally opened with a total of 1200 books. Local guests were invited to attend the silver tea at the opening, drawing nearly 250 guests who supported the new venture. The following day, the XXI Club, one of the first women's clubs in Texas, donated its circulating library to the new library group.

In 1936, due to time constraints and the success of the library, it was decided to elect a board of eight to serve with the Jr. Delphian's library committee. During that year, the library became an adjunct of the city, and Ford Seale was elected the first chairman of the board with Eloise Munson serving as Vice-Chairman. Mr. Seale would serve for several years before retiring, at which time Miss Munson succeeded him as chairman. Muson would serve in that capacity for thrity-two years, until her death in 1969.

In the early years, it was very difficult for the young library to obtain operating funds and new books. Because of this, the

Board voted to ask citizens to call an election to raise taxes to provide for a maintenance and operating fund for the library. Junior Delphians again led the charge, going house to house throughout Denison to obtain signatures for the petition. The election for a two and one-half cent property tax was held on September 15, 1936 and was overwhelmingly approved by local citizens.

During the years following World War II, Millard Cope, a board member and former Denison Herald publisher, created the idea of allowing citizens to donate books to the library in memory of fallen soldiers lost in the war. This program proved to be very successful and many of the books donated throughout the years have been given as memorials.

By 1948, the building was beginning to show its age and one room had to be condemned. The city held a bond election for new school facilities and $100,000 was included for the construction of a new library facility. Miss Munson generously donated the site that the library had been using and the historic home was demolished. Contruction began in September of 1948. The new building was completed and formally opened to the public on May 21, 1950.

In the 1960's, the library once again outgrew its facility and the Board of Directors approved an expansion plan. The library closed from December 14, 1965 to February 1, 1966, when it reopened with the addition of a mezzanine and the capability to hold double the capacity of books and equipment. The mezzanine and renovations were designed by local architect, Donald Mayes.

The original entrance to the 1950 Denison Library Building, ca. 2018.

In 1975, a massive expansion of the library campus was completed with a gift from the Rose Knaur Estate as well as a large grant from the W.B. Munson Foundation. Construction was soon underway when the project was hit wth a combination of delays and spiraling inflation rates.

A Thousand Dollar Club was organized, and all patrons who donated over $1,000 were honored with their names on a plaque at the main entrance to the library. This project, coupled with other fundraising efforts, proved to be enough to complete the construction. This addition and expansion increased the square footage of the library from 8,500 to 18, 356 square feet.

During the expansion, the old entrance to the library on Rusk Avenue was enclosed with a bay window for use as a reading room. The spacious new wing boasted a new entrance on Gandy Street and was hailed as one of the most up-to-date facilities in the state, when it was completed. The library has since undergone several renovations, resulting in one of Denison's most loved gems.

A view showing the 1970's addition to the library and current entrance on Gandy Street, ca. 2018.

Ghost stories of the site go back generations, as many of Denison's book worms have reported seeing a lady walking amongst the stacks and shelves, but when they try to get a better look she vanishes into thin air. Library staff, when left by themselves, have been known to feel the presence of others and have a feeling of being watched. There have even been a few reports of items moving along shelves and across tables.

Who is the Lady of the Library? Is it Miss Eloise, gazing upon her library with wonder? Could it be the spirit of a woman murdered in Denison's Night of Terror? Her home was moved to the site where the 1977 addition now sits. Could she still be roaming around, looking for answers to her unsolved death?

No matter the reasoning, the Lady of the Library has always been viewed as a friendly spirit. The next time you're searching for your favorite book or using the computers, take a stroll amongst the shelves and see if you can spot her.

Chapter
Twenty-One

Justin Raynal
Denison's Benevolent Bachelor

Justin Raynal was born on March 15, 1814 in Bourdeax, France. He immigrated to the U.S. in 1846 with his wife and two children where he became engaged in the jewelry business in New York. He remained there for a short time before moving his family to the Pacific Coast in search of gold. It was at this point that he lost his wife and daughter and became estranged from his son, due to bad behavior on the son's part.

Following California, Raynal moved around to Nevada and "several other states" before arriving in Omaha, Nebraska, where he opened a top-notch restaurant. From there he proceeded to Chicago and was wildly successful in the restaurant business until the Great Chicage Fire occurred in

1871, causing him to lose all that he had worked so hard to gain.

Justin Raynal on January 1, 1879

After the fire, Raynal began making his way to Texas, but ran out of money and had to stop in Springfield, MO where he became a cook at an academy. He saved every penny and moved to Denison in January of 1873 with $100 in his pocket. Ever the entreprenur, in August of 1873, Raynal began construction on a wood frame building measuring 25 by 50 feet at the southwest corner of Main Street and Austin Avenue. This lot is significant in Denison history as it was the first lot sold in the city when the town was laid out. The new restaurant was given the name of The Grand Southern and quickly became one of Denison's most patroned establishments.

The Grand Southern offered the perfect backdrop for Raynal to be able to speak to those in power throughout the city. Justin was a huge supporter of schools and felt that Denison needed an educational facility in order to move forward as a true city. Raynal, who would discuss his ideas with anyone who would listen, often stood atop the bar so he could address the crowd that filled the establishment.

Raynal was deemed as instrumental in the passing of a bond to allow for the first free public graded school in Texas and was heralded as the "white knight" of the public school system. Among his other accomplishments, Raynal served as a City Councilman, Chairman of the Fire Committee, and a member fo the Finance Committee.

In 1878, Raynal puchased the lot to the west of his saloon and contracted with local builder Joseph Koehler to erect a new two-story brick building with dimensions of 24 by 90 feet. Work began on May 5, 1878 and the grand building was completed in January of 1879. Like most buildings of that era, the top cornice displayed the owner's name, in this case Raynal, for all to see.

Justin Raynal died on August 4, 1879 at the Grand Southern, following complications associated with "inflammation of the bowels." He was laid to rest on August 5, 1879 following a large funeral procession that began at the public school on

Main Street and stretched to Oakwood Cemetery on the east side of town.

The Grand Southern, at far left, in 1879.

Organizations present at the funeral included the Maennerehor band, Masons, Gate City Guards, Denison Concert Band, Denison Fire Department, Denison Artillery Company, the Mayor and City Councilman, as well as all public school students and many citizens.

Upon the reading of his will, Raynal left all of his money (totalling nearly $15,000) to the Denison School System. He also bequeathed his brick building at 202 West Main to the school system to be used as an income-producing rental. The only stipulation, and subesqeuntly the last seven words of his will, was "my name to forever remain on cornice."

The school system respected his wishes and the building still retains the Raynal name, although it has undergone several renovations over the years. Raynal Elementary, built in 1891 on the east side of town, was named for him and remained a neighborhood school before its closure in the 1980's.

Raynal Elementary on Denison's East Side, ca. 1895.

A monument was eventually erected on Woodard Street in 1910 to celebrate the amazing gift that Raynal had left to the school system and the city. The monument consisted of Barre granite with a six by six foot base and a height of nearly eighteen feet. In 2007, the monument was struck by a motorist and nearly destoyed. It wold take nearly ten years for funds to be available to restore the monument to its base, where it now resides once more.

The Raynal Monument ca 1940's.

The strange occurrence following the death of Mr. Raynal was discussed in the *Denison Daily News* on September 19, 1879, which reported the following:

"Mr. L. Carr and several other reliable gentlemen tell our reporter a strange story, namely: That the ghost of Justin Raynal was seen Wednesday night.

The young man who received the ghostly visitation occupied the same room that Mr. Raynal died in. Hehas been in Denison only a few weeks, and never saw Mr. Raynal while in the flesh.

It was about midnight when the young man was startled from his slumbers by a noise, as of some one waling in his chamber. He opened his eyes and stared around, and by the fainy light of a lamp, which was partially turned down, he saw a man standing in one corner of the room.

The apparition held in his hands a bundle of papers, and seemed very angry and excited. Twice he went to a trunk, opened and shut it with a slam. The young man supposing that his chamber was invaded bya burglar, sprang from his bed and called for help. The figure then vanished and was seen no more.

The young man describes his ghostly guest, and the description corresponds in every particular with the late Justin Raynal. We will not intrude any of our theories but leave the matter to the conjecture of the reader."

The building where the sighting occurred burned to the ground in 1885 and was replaced by a large brick structure on the same site. The building has been altered over the years and has housed a variety of tenants, but no reports have surfaced of the haunting still continuing.

Could Justin Raynal have left the buidling upon its demise? Or is he still waiting and searching for the papers he looked for that dark night in the 1800's?

The building that replaced the Grand Southern, shown ca. 1950's.

The Raynal Building, ca. 2015. Note the Raynal name still atop the building (at left) despite a new façade.

Chapter Twenty-Two

Gandy Street
The Ghosts of Gandy

321 West Gandy

One of Denison's earliest homes was constructed at 321 West Gandy in 1873. The home was built by local contractor, Joseph Koehler, and was one of the first brick homes built within the city.

Koehler was noted for building Denison's first school as well as the Raynal building which, though altered, still stands today. Sadly, Joseph and his wife only lived in the home a short time before selling due to some financial problems.

The home went through a series of owners and was even owned by local historian, Mavis Anne Bryant, for a time. She had the vision and foresight to do some of the beginning work to help maintain the home's inegrity while attempting to create a plan for bringing it into the present day.

The home was sold before the plans were able to come to fruition, and subsequent owners slowly let the house decay over the years. That all changed in 2009-2010 when this author posted a photo of the home on social media. At this time it was rumored the home would be demolished to make way for a new parking lot for a neighboring rental home.

The home as it appeard shortly after being posted on social media in 2009.

The Hander family purchased the home and made small repairs until myself and my wife moved back to Denison from college. At this point, a massive restoration and addition took place bringing the home from 1000 sqaure feet to 2800 square feet. While much of the home is now new, the historic 1874 structure still stands and has been preserved to showcase the bricks that were made on site as well as the original floors.

The home as it appeared in 2017.

We have lived in the home for over a year and have had no strange occurences...until I opened up a can of worms by beginning this book. This past summer, while working away on the book, we were visited by our friends, Allyson and Kody Stewart.

The way our home is laid out, the master bedroom is upstairs with guest rooms on the main floor. The Stewart's were staying in one of the downstairs rooms that has a view of the french doors leading to the backyard. All seemed normal until one fateful night.

Allyson was awoken by her dogs, something they normally never do, around one o'clock in the morning. Suspecting they needed to go outside, she walked to the french doors and let them out, remaining at the doors so she could watch them. Kody woke up Allyson moved from the bed so he was watching her as she looked out the french doors.

It was at this time that Kody saw a figure, whom he presumed to be myself, walk down the hall and right behind Allyson. When she returned from letting the dogs back in, Kody asked Allyson if I had said anything when he saw me walk by. She replied that no one was in the hall with her and that I hadn't walked past her.

Kody, now very much awake, quickly did a search of the entire house and could find no one. The next morning at breakfast he asked if I had been walking around the previous night. Anyone who knows me, knows I'm prematurely old and go to bed around 9:30 each evening. If I'm awake at 1:30 am it means there has been some sort of nuclear disaster!

This did nothing to ease Kody's mind and everyone in the home was very watchful the next few evenings in case the figure was to show up again. Nothing more has been seen up to this point, but I will admit to having goosebumps as I type this story...in full daylight of course! Was it the spirit of Joseph Koehler, coming back to stay in the dream home he was only able to occupy for a short time? Or was it one of the spirits from the book, making sure their story was told in the correct manner?

1209 West Gandy

W.H. Hall, an assistant superintendent of telegraph for the Katy Railroad moved to Denison in the early part of 1909. He began work on a large eight room house at 1209 West Gandy on May 30, 1909 with an estimated cost of $2, 750. The large four-square home was sided in cypress from Jefferson, Texas and was one of the finest homes in Denison upon completion.

Mr. Hall seems to have excelled at his chosen profession because in 1910 he was named superintendent of the telgraph office. It was noted in the article that Hall had been with the Katy since graduating from college and had worked his way up from a clerk.

An interesting fact of Mr. Hall is that he was quite talented with electrical components, even going so far as to have met Thomas Edison in the early part of the 20th century. They became good friends and Hall would often take trips to Edison's laboratory in Orange, New Jersey.

The Hall home, shown one house to the left of the corner house, in a postcard used to showcase the beauty of Denison's residences.

It is said that Mrs. Hall was afraid to be left alone in the house, often having difficulty while William was away. As a solution, Hall had the entire house wired with an Edison bulb at the top of each wall. They were in every room of the house, and should Mrs. Hall have gotten spooked, she simply had to turn on the lights with a master switch that she had at her disposal. It is believed this is the first type of lit-home security ever used in a residential structure.

There were two fires reported in the home pretty close together. In 1925, the fire department was called to the home due to an electric fuse blowing, causing an alarm. Firefighters were on the scene fast enough that no damage resulted. Later that same year, a cleaning cloth used on the floor caught fire and threatened trouble. The fire was quickly extinguished with a small loss to the interior of the room where the fire originated.

The home went through a few owners before becoming the long-time home of the Ontiveros family. Under the direction of the latest generation, the home has been restored to its early-day splendor and continues to grace one of Denison's most prominent residential blocks.

A home as large and as storied as this is usually going to have a tale or two of strange happenings. The current owners, Paul and Kim Ontiveros, of the home have shared several videos on social media that indicate a spirit may be in their home. A small orb is seen flying through various rooms, often going quite fast. There have been several instances of this occuring, sometimes in different rooms as well.

The Hall-Ontiveros home at present.

One of the instances involves a clock that used to belong to Kim's grandmother. Several months ago, Kim noticed that the clock, which normally sits on a shelf in their parlor, was turned around. Thinking nothing of it, she turned it back around and went about her day. Strangely enough, for the next three mornings, each time she went into the parlor the same clock was turned around again.

The clock that belonged to Kim Ontiveros' grandmother.

On a recent day, Paul noticed that the clock was turned halfway around. Upon turning it to again face forward, he noticed the time was different. The clock no longer works so the couple have always left it set at twelve o'clock. However, something had changed the clock to where it know was set at three. Neither Paul not Kim had touched the time on the clock, leaving them to believe that it was another entitity all together.

Who is the spirit that haunts the large house on Gandy? Is it Mrs. Hall? Forever fearful of being left alone, it is possible that even in death she stays with her home in the hopes of having company. Whomever the spirit may be, it does lead for interesting discussion for Paul and Kim.

Chapter Twenty-Three

Sears Street

The Sears Street Specter

There is a home on Sears Street that is said to have a spirit that lingers. The home, located at 1210 West Sears, was built sometime around 1906 and was the scene of many parties throughout the years, especially Halloween parties which were the favorite of the lady who lived there.

It is mentioned in newspapers from the time that the house would be decorated with all manner of ghoulish jackolanterns and was lit by the light of hundreds of candles. The guests arrived in cotume and one of the highlights of the parties was the fortune teller that could tell guests how they may prosper, as well as how they may meet their demise.

Over the years, the home passed through various owners until it was purchased by Gary Sewell. Work quickly commenced to rid the home of the "udpates" that had been done over the years. One of these updates was the addition of a drop-down ceiling from a height of ten feet down to eight feet.

1210 West Sears, ca. 2018.

Gary worked to take the ceiling down by using a saw that he plugged into an outlet, but quickly ran into problems. The saw would rev up and work well, but would suddenly stop and not restart. He would then move the cord to a different plug and had similar results. The electricity was checked and there were no problems with it, and the saw passed inspection as well without any findings. Could some entity have been messing with the power…trying to prevent anymore work from happening at the house?

The strange occurances didn't stop there though. A painter was hired by the Sewell's to completley paint the interior of the home. When the painter got to the front living room he opened all of the windows and doors to help with circulation. Just when he was about to start, all of the doors slammed shut and all windows closed on their own.

The frightened painter tried with all of his might to get out, but was truly locked in the front room. He was eventually able to pry a door open and fled from the home, never to return, even leaving his tools and other equipment behind.

The final occurance involved the center stairwell that is found inside the home. The stairs lead to a small room, no larger than an attic. One evening, Mr. Sewell saw someone running up the stairs followed by a basketball rolling down each step from the top down to the main entryway. Upon investigation, there was no one at the room at the top of the stairs and no one else in the home.

Who is the spirit that lingers at the bright little house on Sears Street? What do they want? Is it possbile they have since moved on, no longer remaining to haunt the home?

Chapter Twenty-Four

Clowning Around
It's All Fun and Games...

Evil or demonic clowns are not necessarily new to society. The creepy characters have appeared in Edgar Allen Poe's works as well as several 19th century European plays.

The modern clown character was made popular by Stephen King's novel, *It,* which was the first novel to introduce the fear of an evil clown in modern culture. In the novel, the clown is a monster which feeds mainly on children after luring them and then assuming whatever shape the children find most terrifying.

In late 2016, the South was gripped by a clown epidemic. The nightmareish clowns appeared throughout North and South

Carolina, Georgia, Alabama, and even right here in Denison. Reports varied from state to state but the recurrent theme was that clowns were seen around town with several trying to lure children into the woods. These clown sightings sparked nationwide panic with some cities going so far as to ban clown costumes within their limits.

The evil-looking clown spotted at Forest Park in 2015.

In Denison, clowns were spotted over the course of several weeks. Local police responded to reports of two clowns lurking beneath the viaduct downtown and another respoded to a call of a clown in the 300 block of Lillis Lane that chased a young man. One clown was seen consistently throughout the city, always in the same outfit and always with a handful of balloons. Several photos were captured of the clown waiting on a bench in Forest Park and lurking at the entrance to Waterloo Lake.

Local news stations ran stories about the spooky sightings, with local police urging citizens to take caution while traveling in the city and to report any odd behavior or clowns lurking around. Just as quickly as they had appeared, the clowns vanished. Although, some still claim to see the creepy clown holding balloons at various intersections and parks, causing citizens to always be on their guard.

Another creepy clown figure at Waterloo Park in 2015.

Were the appearances just one big hoax brought on by people's fear of clowns? Were they just youngsters looking to get a laugh? Or was it something more sinister...?

Chapter
Twenty-Five

B. McDaniel Middle School
The Man at the Middle School

Since the city's founding, Denison has always had some of the most modern and advanced school buildings in the state. In the early days, new elementary schools and additions to the Senior High School were common sights around town. This innovation and growth saw the creation of a new Senior High School in the 1950's, with the old building utilized as a Junior High.

Denison soon outgrew the old structure and in the early 1960's, the decision was made to build a second Junior High on the west side of town. Local leading architect Donald

Mayes designed a large campus to be equipped with the latest technology and educational materials.

The all-new junior high was to be located on a forty-acre site bounded by Crawford Street, Lillis Lane, and Jennie Lane. The building was completed in 1964 and was named for long-time superintendent of schools, Mr. Hughes. During the 1980's, the name of the school was changed to B. McDaniel Junior High following the consolidation of many of Denison's schools.

Teachers and students at the school have reported doors opening and closing on their own and school supplies falling from the shelves when no one else is around. Often, a door leading into a certain art class would open on its own during the middle of class, sending whispers of someithng otherworldy amongst the aspiring young artists. While the spirit has never been seen, it has always been assumed that it is the spirit of a man, with many assuming it to be either Hughes or McDaniel.

Chapter
Twenty-Six

The Barrett Building
All that Remains of an Empire

For many years, Denison's YMCA was the pride and joy of the city. The organization was originally located upstairs in the 300 block of West Woodard Street, but quickly outgrew the site within just a few decades. Property was eventually purchased in the early 1920's and a basement was constructed on the lot ond covered over until a more formal building could be erected.

The venerable building, known today as the Barrett Building, was originally constructed in the mid-1920's for use as a YMCA. W.S. Hibbard was appointed president with George Morgan serving as vice president, A. Loret acting as recording secretary, H.G. Howe functioning as treasurer, and J.E. Morris completing the group as general secretary.

An early rendering of the Denison Y.M.C.A. that appeared in the Dallas Morning News in 1919.

The new edifice opened in 1925 and contained 45 sleeping rooms, in addtion to an auditorium, gymnasium, men's room, offices, gamerooms, and the ladies' room. Other interesting amenities included a two lane bowling alley, a reading room, as well as social rooms.

Tragedy struck the YMCA on December 18, 1926 when a boiler exploded, injuring James Morris Jr., J.E. Morris, and an African American porter.

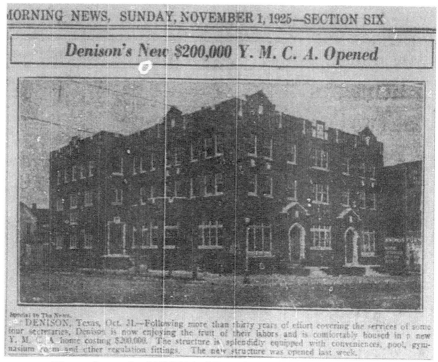

The newly completed YMCA building, shortly after its grand opening.

The explosion would prove to have fatal consequences. The following appeared in the *Denison Herald*:

3 Hurt when Boiler Bursts
"Explosion Rocks and Damages Denison Y.M.C.A Building

James Morris Jr. was seriously scalded and otherwise injured, his father J.E. Morris general secretary of the Y.M.CA. and a negro porter were severely injured when a boiler in the Y.M.C.A Building here exploded Saturday evening. The large brick and steel building was rocked by the explosion that was heard for several blocks.

Partitions of tile and brick were blown from their places, pipes ripped from the structure, with broken glass and framework scattered and twisted in the boiler room over a section of the basement.

Boilermakes had been employed on boiler repair work Saturday afternoon. The boiler was reported ready for service and fired up. Attention was attracted to the boiler and J.E. Morris, secretary, with his son and a negro porter, went to the boiler room. They started to remove the fire from under the boiler when the explosion occurred. James Morris Jr, 19, was blown to the floor and boiling water spread over his body and debris completely covered him. His fatherwas blown against a partition and stunned, being partly covered with wreckage when firemen arrived.

Firemen answering the alarm worked ten minutes before rescuing young Morris, and he was carried to the City Hopsital, where attending physicians said he was seriously injured.

It is believed the safety valve on the boiler stuck, sausing the trouble. The boiler was wrecked, as were the water and gas pipes. Boys playing basketball on the court in the gymnasium were blown from their feet by the concussion. The building was not damaged greatly above the basement. The walls were not cracked. The greatest damage being confined to a section where the boilers were located and adjoining walls."

That article was followed by one from the *Dallas Morning News* on December 21, 1926.

Victim of Denison Y.M.C.A Blast Dies

"James E. Morris Jr., 19, who was injured Saturday evening when a steam boiler in the local Y.M.C.A. exploded, died in the city hopsital Monday evening. He was the son of Mr. and Mrs. J.E. Morris. His father was secretary of the Y.M.C.A. where the accident occurred. Funeral services will be held at the Waples Memorial Methodist Church at 3 o'clock Wednesday afternoon.

The accident that resulted in the death of the young man did several thousand dollars damage to the Y.M.C.A. building and resulted from a cut-off valve from the boiler to the radiator sytem being closed. Young Morris was a student at Austin College, being a graduate of the Denison High School two years ago. He was a member of the Denison De Molay Chapter. Others injured when the accident occurred suffered only slight bruises."

Flemming Foods gained control of the building in 1937, after the YMCA closed, and operated their headquarters for the Kraft-Phenix Cheese Corporation at the site for several years. Although used as a headquarters, Kraft allowed the pool to remain open throughout the 1940's, preserving a popular place for Denison's youth to swim.

Entrepreneur and pharmacist, Jack Barrett, arrived in the Denison area in 1939 to launch a multi-store Piggly Wiggly system that would prove to be vastly profitable. Barrett purchased the Piggly Wiggly at 507 West Main Street and established stores in Sherman, Madill, Durant, Paris, Hugo, and Greenville.

Barrett purchased the imposing YMCA building at the corner of Main Street and Mirick Avenue in 1948, following the relocation of the Kraft Food Co. from the building to a new headquarters site. He quickly added his name atop the building, and it has been known ever since as the Barrett Building.

The YMCA building as it appeared shortly before being purchased by Jack Barrett.

In 1960, Barrett announced the transfer of all of his grocery store holdings to the Piggly Wiggly Corporation of Jacksonville, Florida. The amount of the sale was never disclosed, but was rumored to have run into the millions of dollars, with Barrett retaining the real estate.

Barrett Drug, a long time Denison institution, was established in the basement of the Barrett Building at the time of the grovery store transfer. The basement area, which had once been the YMCA swimming pool, underwent an extensive remodeling to make way for the new store. The store, when open, was going to have enough merchandise to make it a small department store.

Space on one of the upper floors was also remodeled into a luxurious apartment for Mr. Barrett and his wife, Cecil Davis Barrett. The 15- room residence featured a fame room, a library and cocktail room, kitchen and dining areas, and three bedroom suites, each with their own bathroom ensuite. One unique feature of the Barrett apartment is the large glass panels between each room that allow light to pass from one side of the apartment to the other when all of the shades are raised.

The drug store started to gain some traction in the local economy, and soon an addition was planned directly to the east in a site formerly occupied by a bus terminal. This addition was designed by Donald Mayes and featured a playful arcaded entrance along Main Street with a monumental neon sign across much of the façade. Formal dedication of the expanded store occurred in May of 1966 with over 25,000 square feet of space.

In 1976, Barrett purchased, remodeled, and renovated buildings at 517-519 West Main, the longtime home of Jennings Furniture. A building at 515 West Main was also remodeled, adding 7,500 sqaure feet of retail in addition to vast amounts of storage space in the upstairs lofts. These monumental remodels and additions would earn Barrett's the title of a true Denison commercial empire.

Jack Barrett passed away in February of 1968, and the company was transferred tohis wife, Cecile D. Barrett, who managed the company until her death on January 6, 1989. The heirs of Mrs. Barrett elected to let the employees, number at nigh 80 on staff, buy out the company to continue with the Barrett name.

Barrett Drug as it appeared with the Mayes-designed addition and eye-catching neon signs.

Several recent occupants of the Barrett Building and the structures adjacent have reported seeing Mr. Barrett walking throughout the halls. Others have reported cold spots throughout the buildings and hair raising occurences when they are by themselves, leading many to believe that Mr. Barrett may still be around watching over his former business and those who have come to occupy the building since.

Chapter

Twenty-Seven

Historic Denison High School
The Spirit that Lingered

Denison has long boasted of a fantastic educational system, seconded by none in this part of the country. From our city's very inception, education has always played a vital role for our citizens, beginning with the first free graded public school in the State of Texas.

In Denison's early days, as has been previously discussed in this book, debate raged on whether to use the young city's tax system to build a new jail or a new school. With public figures such as Justin Raynal firmly backing the school proposal, the citizens were swayed and $20,000 in bonds was issued to build Denison's first true school.

A site at the 700 block of West Main was selected and the new school, christened The Educational Institute, was erected in 1873. It was claimed that the school, under the direction of Professor Phillips, had a constant attendance of 530 scholars by 1875.

The school was later renamed the Washington School and served the city well before it was replaced by Denison's grand high school in 1913-1914. Noted architect, Arthur Osborne Watson, of Austin, Texas, did the design for the new structure. The new building was far larger than the previous one, and was to be built at the same site, but slightly in front of the old structure so as not to impede classes during construction.

$110,000 High School Building, Denison, Texas.

—Photo by Robinson.

A view of the new Denison High School during construction. The Washington School, Denison's first school, stands at far left. Ca. 1913.

The new design called for a three-story brick building in a genius blend of Italian Romanesque, Mission Revival, and Prairie styles. The cream-colored building boasted a clay tile hipped roof with broad overhanging eaves and a bell tower with clock that was viewable from many locations around Denison.

An expansion took place in 1927 with a design from noted Dallas architect, Mark Lemmon. A new wing was added on the south side of the building that housed additional classrooms and a large gymnasium. In 1939, the school received another expansion to the north that created an immense 1500-seat auditorium and classroom wing in the Art Deco style. This addition was possible through the auspices of the Federal Works Progress Administration.

A view of the historic Denison High School, ca. 1950's.

The school building served Denison for generations before it was deemed too small, and was replaced by a new school on the south side of the city in 1954. The old high school was renamed the McDaniel Junior High School, in honor of longtime Denison Superintendent B. McDaniel. In 1956, the balcony portion of the auditorium was closed in, creating six new classrooms on the third floor.

Eventually deemed to be obsolete, the building saw its last class of students in 1986, when all students were moved to the newer Junior High that had been built on Denison's west side several years before. It was at this time that the building, once the most prominent structure along Denison's historic Main Street, became vacant and slowly decayed into a state of disrepair.

Denison Heritage Inc., a local non-profit formed to preserve the historic Denison High School and other local historic sites, purchased the campus in the summer of 2001 from the Denison Independent School District. Work quickly began with $100,000 spent to help with roof leaks, a fence around the property to keep trespassers out, and plexi-glass installations in some of the broken windows to allow for light and ventilation in the cavernous structure.

Fundraisers were held with the hopes that the gymnasium and south wing of the building could be demolished to expose some of the fantastic architecture that had been hidden for a number of years. Items such as lockers, desks, light fixtures, and tin ceiling tiles were auctioned off with the hopes of raising much-needed funds to preserve the building.

Despite the best intentions of Denison Heritage Inc. members, and their tireless efforts to raise funds, time passed by and work began to slow on the historic structure. In 2007, Mayor Robert Brady and the Denison City Council voted to demolish the historic structure at a cost of $500,000 with grants from both the Smith and Munson Foundations.

Demolish began in such a way that the newer wings and additions to the school were demolished first, revealing key pieces of the original structure that had been hidden for decades. Torrential rains slowed demolition before the main structure was touched, giving a new grassroots group, Save Denison History, time to try and save what was left of the structure and turn it into an events center and office building for downtown.

Despite monetary pledges in the millions and huge amounts of outcry from the local community, the Council ultimately decided to proceed with demolition. The historic building that had graced downtown Denison for nearly a century came tumbling down, leaving many with a feeling of despair and a sense that the city had lost part of its soul.

Since that time, the large lot that housed Denison's premier building has been vacant, leaving a large gap in Denison's historic business district. However, recent plans have been unveiled that call for the lot to become a large park that could be used by the entire community. The hope is that both the building and former students can be recognized in some way in the future design, showing the Denison does not forget our heritage and its importance in our everyday lives.

One of the best fundraisers that the building was used for, prior to demolition, was playing host to a haunted house, put on by the Denison Jaycee's. The inside of the eerie structure was made into the stuff of nightmares. Adults and children alike would line up along Main Street for their chance to get to go in and make it through the "haunted" structure.

Several stories told by volunteers of the haunted house and guests suggest that maybe more than just the cheap scare was at work in the building. Some of the volunteers claimed to feel strange presences when setting up the haunted house and seeing figures walking in rooms that were not in use at the time. Upon investigation, no one could be found. Guests said they sometimes felt unseen arms on their backs or shoulders, pulling on them as if trying to get them deeper into the building. Some were so frightened that they did not come back for future years' activities.

While the building was being demolished, many went to photograph the structure to preserve images of what it once looked like. The author went, like so many, to capture the final months of the building's life and its ultimate demise. One of the photos turned out to show what appears to be a figure standing at the main entrance of the historic structure. Three photos of this entrance were taken at the same time, but only one shows the figure. Could alumni from the historic school have been guarding it all the years that it was there? If so, did they leave when it was demolished or are they still present along Denison's Main Street? Only time will tell.

The figure at the main entrance to the historic Denison High School, ca. 2007.

Chapter
Twenty-Eight

Lake Texoma
Lights on the Lake

The Red River has always been a force of nature for North Texas. Seasonal floods were a common sight for much of the Texoma area that could often be devastating for area farmers and businesses such as railroads. One of the greatest floods occurred in the early 1900's and completely washed away one of the Katy Railroads' train bridges, causing major delays in services.

With all of these constant fluctuations, local leaders began to see the need for some form of flood control for the raging river. For many years, appeals were made to the government to try to start work on what would become known as the Denison Dam.

A preliminary sketch of the Denison Dam as it was expected to appear after construction.

The good news finally came on June 29, 1939, when the Denison Herald ran a special edition of the paper bearing the news that congress had approved $5,000,000 to start construction of the dam. Celebrations were held around town and an impromptu parade took place along Main Street. Denison truly had arrived and was heralded as "the Best Town by a Dam Site!"

In total, over one hundred thousand acres would be cleared to make way for the massive Lake Texoma that would be impounded by the dam. Railroad tracks had to be relocated, new highway bridges added, and the Cumberland oil field preserved. In addition, several towns were completely abandoned to make way for the rising waters of the lake. These towns included Hagerman and Preston, Texas and Alyesworth and Woodville, Oklahoma.

Once completed, the Denison Dam was the largest earthen-rolled dam in the world, creating Lake Texoma, with an astounding 550 miles of shoreline. The total cost for the project would rise to $54 million by the time the project came to completion.

The massive water intake under construction for the new Denison Dam.

Preston, Texas was a prominent trading destination located along the Red River and was a popular crossing for the Butterfield Stage Lines and the Shawnee cattle trail. The small town flourished until the Missouri, Kansas & Texas railroad bypassed the town to the east, isolating the town and her citizens.

Hagerman, Texas was originally known as Steedman but was renamed in 1909 when the railroad ran a line through the town. James Hagerman was a railroad attorney at that time so it is possible that the citizens renamed the town in order to entice the railroad to make them a stop along the line. Sadly, the population never grew to what town leaders hoped and was around 150 when the dam was built.

Woodville, Oklahoma was named after a prominent Chickasaw citizen, Judge L Lipscomb Wood. Once hailed as the first town in Indian Territory and a popular destination for Bonnie and Clyde, the town ultimately succumbed to the floodwaters, becoming an underwater ghost town.

One of the more macabre operations that took place for the new lake was the removal of bodies from cemeteries to relocate them to cemeteries outside of the flood plain. In total, over three thousand bodies from forty-nine cemeteries were to be disinterred and reburied in eleven new graveyards that were created for the Corp of Engineers. The grave relocation would take almost a year to complete.

In 2011, following months of drought, the lake levels were low enough that some of the old headstones and building foundations could be seen along the ever-growing shoreline. While the bodies had been removed and the towns cleared of their residents, many of the tombstones were left in the cemeteries and the buildings abandoned, creating strange underwater cities.

For years, locals from both Oklahoma and Texas have reported seeing strange orb-like lights dancing across the waters of Lake Texoma. The lights are best observed at night and seem to be concentrated over areas where the sunken towns are located. Varying in colors and size, the orbs are said to be hauntingly beautiful.

While many of the graves from the towns were removed, is it possible that some of the spirits remained in their hometowns? Could some graves have been missed completely and the lights are the spirits of the forgotten? The next time you go to the lake for a night cruise, be sure to watch for the lights on the lake and think of those ghost towns that still dwell beneath the surface of the water.

Chapter
Twenty-Nine

Memorial Hospital
The Patients that Never Left

In 1959, it was determined that Denison may need a new medical facility to better serve its growing population. The Denison Area Chamber of Commerce created a Hosptal Subcomittee which met with the Denison City Council to commission a study by Ross Garrett Associates, an esteemed hospital consulting firm, to assess the medical care needs of the area.

The need was found, and in 1961 the Denison Hospital Authority was created by a City Ordinance and charged with the duty of building a new hospital facility. On April 17th of that year, the Authority engaged Page Southerland Page, an

Austin-based firm,to be the architects of the new medical facility.

A 14-acre tract of land was acquired for the new hospital through an agreement with the Katy Employees Hospital Association, which had been in Denison since the early part of the 20th century. A fundraising campaign quickly began with the institution of a Thousand Dollar Club, with hopes of getting 100 members.

Fundraising and various other efforts were successful and in 1963 bids were opened in the main banquet room of the Hotel Denison with over 200 people in attendance. A bid was successfully awarded and a groundbreaking ceremony for the new hospital took place on March 24, 1963.

Denison's Memorial Hosptial opened in 1965 as a small community hospital to serve both Denison citizens and Katy Railroad employees. The official opening ceremony was held on March 24, 1965 with over 8,000 people in attendance. Originally the hospital had 84 beds and a staff of 145, serving 1500 patients during its first year of operation.

Memorial Hospital shortly after completion.

The hospital quickly gained noteriety throughout the Texoma area as a place for unparalleled medical care. In 1968 fundraising began for an expansion, and in 1970 the third floor and a new Intensive Care Unit were completed and opened. This was followed quickly in 1971 by the opening of the Eloise Munson Radiation Center, named for a local philanthropist, for the treatment of cancer.

In 1976, the name of the hospital was officially changed from Memorial Hosptial to Texoma Medical Center. This change was in part due to the hospital's transition from a small community hospital to a regional hospital serving a large population. That same year, a 24-hour emergency room and an office building, the Texoma Medical Plaza Physician's Office Building, were opened at the existing facility.

Of interesting note, when the hospital changed its name, it was decided that a special symbol should go along with the name update. The approved design has a pair of hands (symbolizing skill and human contact) encircling a heart (representing human warmth and compassion) superimposed on a cross (the universal sign for healthcare). The new symbol, meant to promise patrons of the hopsital quality healthcare with a patient's needs as the foremost consideration, is still used today and reflects the hospital's preservation and recognition of its past.

In 1977 the Denison Hospital Authority officially acquired Madonna Hospital from Madonna, Inc., changing the name to TMC East. A year later, a $7.5 million expansion to the TMC campus created a new north wing for the facility.

An early view of Memorial Hospital.

In typical fashion, the successful facility kept growing and with that growth came the addition of cutting-edge medical equipment to better serve the Texoma area. The 1980's saw the addition of the Peggy Munson Wilcox Trauma Center, the Lattimore Special Care Unit, and the Eloise Munson Angiographic Laboratory.

The Texoma Medical Center Foundation was created in 1982 in order to continue fundraising efforts for the hospital. Satellite clinics were added in Whitesboro, Whtiewright, and Pottsboro, and in 1985 TMC purchased the Katy Hospital from the Katy Employee's Hospital Association. This merger made TMC, with 300 patient beds, larger than 90 percent of the general acute hospitals in Texas.

The hospital continued to fluorish and grow over the years with the addition of a new medical building, known as the Morrison Medical Building, that housed various physician's offices. The 1990's also saw special attention given to the hospital from none other than Reba McEntire.

Reba hosted several concerts in Denison, often bringing other high-list celebrities, in order to raise money and awareness for families that may need a helping hand while their loved ones are in the hospital. From these fundraising efforts, Reba's Ranch House was born, offering families a place to stay that was near the hospital without ever asking for any payment for services rendered during their stay.

Due to changes in healthcare, the hospital began to look for a buyer to change the medical center from non-profit to a for-profit facility, Universal Health Services, Inc. The new company took over operations of TMC and began work on a new $200 million dollar facility along highway 75 in Denison in 2009.

The new eight-story hospital tower opened to great fanfare and has become an assset for the local community. A new Reba's Ranch House was contructed close by as well as a new physician's building. TMC recently completed the addition of a new four-story tower that includes a large expansion to the Emergency Department. With the new expansion and quality healthcare, TMC has proved it is going to remain a strong asset for Denison and the surrounding area.

The former Texoma Medical Center building that served the area for so long, is being torn down to make way for something new. This is the building that we will focus on as it has a number of hauntings that occurred throughout its existence.

View of the former TMC as demolition begins on the massive structure.

View of the former TMC as demolition begins on the massive structure.

Nurses and patients alike have long said that the old facility was haunted by those who never left. There are even some claims that former physicans, long deceased, were known to lurk around the various hallways and corridors.

One common occurrence that would happen, especially to nurses on night duty, were lights coming on in empty rooms and call buttons going off in areas that had no patients to press them. Nurses would often go check these rooms, see that no one was in there, and simply turn off the lights or call alarms that had gone off. There was a general understanding that it was wandering spirits and no fuss was ever made.

Most activity seemed pretty subdued until the facility closed, that's when things seem to have gotten extra spooky. Several employees that took photos of the interior of the building as momentos claim they can see faces of former patients in the glass partitions throughout the hospital. Some of the people in the photos were positively identified as both patients and former medical staff.

One photo that we do have was taken by the daughter of an administrator while she was home from college. Driving around the facility, she noticed a light on, although there was not supposed to be any electricity at the old facility. She snapped some photos to show her mom, but inadvertantly may have photographed one of the window spirits. There is a face that can be made out in the window that was identified as a former employee of the facility that had passed away a number of years before.

The photo of a former office of the old TMC shows what appears to be a face at center between the blinds.

The final instance that we will write about involves several members of the same family that had gone to the hospital to help clean out the remainder of the furniture from the old ICU. This part of the facility was shaped like a horseshoe with rooms numbered from one to thirteen. While the three were moving furniture they noticed one of the call-lights came on in one of the rooms.

A call was quickly made to the IT department at the new hospital and it was determined that there was no way the light could have gone off, all connections had been severed. As soon as the phone call ended, all call-lights began going off from room one all the way to room thirteen, frightening all three men so much that they left the facility.

Chapter

Thirty

The Cotton Mill
The Faces in the Flames

The Denison Cotton Mill began in the 1880's when the Denison Manufacturing Company began work on a large building on the far southern edge of Denison. The site chosen for the new mill consisted of six and one-half acres that were donated to the company by a local real estate group with the promise that a structure be erected on the property. This piece of land would later become known as 701 West Rice Street.

Work progressed quickly and on October 14, 1890, local newspapers reported that the last floor had been completed on the structure.

The new mill was hailed as the largest such facility west of the Mississippi, covering an astounding 152,000 square feet of manufacturing space with an additional 40, 0000 square feet of warehouse space.

The four-story brick structure was constructed by Henry L Breneman of Paris, Texas and took an army of masons and other laborers to complete, costing nearly $500,000 at completion. Another source notes that work was awarded to W.C. Green of Chicago, who relocated a steam brick making plant from Kansas to Denison in order to furnish enough brick for the mammoth building.

Upon completion, the brick and stone-trimmed structure was 300 feet long and 100 feet wide with four stories and a basement. On either end was a five-story tower with a six-story tower built on the back of the building to house the elevator and its machinery. In addition to the main building, there was a two-story repair shop and a boiler room housing eight boilers.

The main building had 650 windows, each an impressive six feet by ten feet. There was also a well with a capacity of 200,000 gallons of water per day, and the building was lit with over 600 incandescent electric lights.

The manufacturing group, said to consist of New England interests, was poised for greatness. However, the fledgling company was ultimately doomed and production never took off.

In January of 1892, the operation was taken over by the Denison Rolling Mill Company and was succeeded on March 22, 1894 by the Red River Cotton Manufacturing Company. Next in the long line of owners was the American Cotton

Spinning Company, incorporated August 12, 1899, with capital stock of $100,000.

The Denison Cotton Mill ca 1890

The Denison Cotton Mill ca 1890.

The seemingly rough start to the mill ended in 1905, when the Munson family purchased the operation and formed the Denison Cotton Mill Company. The company was officially incorporated on August 5, 1905, with W. B. Munson serving as president.

The cotton mill flourished under the leadership of the Munson family, eventually employing 300 people to handle daily operations. Employees built homes, churches, and a school around the mill, creating one of the largest unincorporated towns, referred to as Cotton Mill, in Texas. The area was eventually annexed into Denison in the late 1950's.

During 1937, the mill produced 4.2 million yards of cotton duck material ranging from 19 to 72 inches wide. The cloth, known for its quality, was marketed throughout the United States under the brands of Great Mallard, Dreadnaught, and Pacific Ducks.

Typical homes of workers surrounding the cotton mill.

During World War II, the plant received the Army-Navy "E" rating and produced duck for the armed forces in addition to its regular business.

The mill closed in 1977 with the hope that the facility could serve the area in another way. A group of Dallas investors purchased the plant but plans never came to fruition and the building remained vacant.

On October 29 1982, a neighboring woman was awoken by a bright red sky and the smell of smoke. The historic cotton mill was fully engulfed in flames with flames and smoke pouring out of every window. All local fire departments and auxiliary firefighters were called to the scene, but it was not enough to save the structure. At dawn all the remained standing was the old smokestack, the plant water tower, and a portion of the southeast section of brick walls.

Many locals from around the area turned out to see the fire that devastated a portion of the city and forever removed one of Denison's landmarks from the city's landscape. Several onlookers took photos of the burning relic to document the scene. Some say that you could see the silhouettes of people standing in the large windows as the flames devoured the massive structure.

The Denison Cotton Mill as it burned in October of 1982.

Many believed that the spirits in the windows were former employees of the Cotton Mill, forever working away at the institution that built their community. Whatever they were, it is possible they could still remain in the area, watching over their beloved Cotton Mill Community.

THE END

....OR IS IT?

Made in the USA
Middletown, DE
02 September 2024

60235713R00130